CANDLE ART

CANDLE ART

A Gallery of Candle Designs & How to Make Them

With 16 Color Plates and 115 Photographs by the Author

by RAY SHAW

William Morrow & Company, Inc. / New York / 1973

Printed in the United States of America.

Library of Congress Catalog Card Number 73-5324

Designed by Ann Mezey
Frontispiece: Foliating candle.

To Dr. Blanche Weill
who lights a candle wherever she finds darkness

· Acknowledgments ·

I shall always be indebted to the masters whose paintings first made me aware of the beauty, magic and mystery of candlelight. I am also grateful to the following friends and acquaintances who have posed for the photographs in this book or allowed me to use their candles as illustrations: Mrs. John Bayha, Arnold Miller, Alfred Pantzer, Rita Santoroski, Angel and John Scarpa, Lyle Schultz, and the friends at Candle Cupboard Products, The Candle Shop, M. & R. Candle Crafts and The Candle Cottage.

· Contents ·

· List of Color Plates ·

·Introduction·

Man has always been fascinated by fire and light. In the beginning the world about him was engulfed in darkness save for an unfamiliar sun and those mysterious night visitors, the moon and the stars. Only the flame of the primitive torch lighted man's first steps out of the darkness. Made of dried branches or rushes dipped in suet, the torch may well have been the original candle. The idea might have come to primitive man when he first observed how bright a light was given off by the burning fat of the meat he cooked over the open fire.

No one knows exactly how long ago man used this portable source of illumination, but he would come to pray, study, invent, record history and create masterpieces of music, art and literature—all to the flicker of the candle, Homer's "light of heaven."

Ancient Egyptian reliefs depict candles; and archaeologists have found candlesticks that date as far back as 2500 B.C., to the great Minoan civilization that then flourished on the isle of Crete.

Early mention of the candle is found in the Bible. Moses was commanded to make a golden candlestick; and when King Solomon built the Temple he had five candlesticks at the south end and five at the north of the holy sanctuary.

The Roman scholar and historian Pliny referred to Greek candles in the first century A.D. And it is believed that the Romans first used candles made of rope dipped in pitch.

By the Middle Ages the use of the candle had become so extensive that candlemakers' guilds were established. The soft flickering of tall tapers lighted the palaces of the rich and gave special meaning to religious ceremonies. For the common man, however, the candle remained a luxury, and he continued to rely on the rush dipped in suet for illumination.

The bee, the first wax manufacturer, made an important contribution to candlemaking. While more expensive than tallow, beeswax gave off a pleasant, aromatic fragrance rather than the offensive odor of burning fat. Vegetable waxes, such as the wax that comes from the bayberry shrub or tree used by the American colonists, also became popular.

The growth of America's whaling industry after the Revolutionary War introduced yet another material: spermaceti, a solid, waxy substance obtained from the sperm whale. Because it was odorless and did not soften or bend in the summer heat, spermaceti gained immediate popularity.

The nineteenth century saw a number of advances in candlemaking. The plaited candle wick gave a brighter and more even light, and a colorless, odorless substance, paraffin, was introduced.

Old in time, the candle flame is ever new in the way it transforms a room, an event, a face. A dinner is more festive by candlelight; no birthday cake is complete without it. Candles are used in the rituals of virtually every religion. Christmas is a time for candles; Chanukah is the Festival of Lights; and Dewali, India's colorful autumn holiday, is celebrated in a blaze of flickering flames.

Down through the ages and in all the families of man, the glow of a candle symbolizes peace, serenity and warmth. Its radiance brings another dimension to the humblest dwelling and its soft flame creates a mood of friendliness and Old World charm. It seems fitting and natural that today, with our newly aroused awareness of our creative power and unexplored potential, we turn to the art of candlemaking.

You too can shape a piece of wax into a thing of beauty, and you don't need a special studio or any elaborate equipment. You can do it right in your own kitchen. Look at the collection of candles on page 63. The shapes and molds of many of these can be found in your home. Candlemaking materials are easily available today and invite you to an experience in the exciting world of form, light and color.

The step-by-step instructions in this book will tell you how to make over 55 different types of candles. As you become familiar with the materials and master the fundamentals of candlemaking, you will be ready to express your own unique self. Then let your imagination run riot! Create unusual shapes and never-before-seen decorations.

You can make candles for your own delight, to give as gifts or even to sell. What may begin as a spare-time hobby or diversion might in time develop into a commercial venture. After you master the basic techniques, you can begin to use your imagination and inventiveness to gain profitable results.

You will probably spread around the fruits of your labors as gifts to relatives and friends. As your reputation grows, you may receive requests for made-to-order candles. You might then begin to consider making candles for profit while staying right in your own kitchen.

A couple I know recently became interested in candlemaking and secured for themselves a free vacation by instructing hundreds of bored passengers on a cruise ship in the art of candlemaking. Two neighbors of mine, each with small children, formed a partnership and are giving candlemaking demonstrations in department stores and are teaching teen-age groups and adult-education classes in their workshop. You can obtain publicity by giving talks on candlemaking to women's clubs and church groups, or by placing an occasional advertisement in your local newspaper.

Beginners tend to underprice their products. Don't you do it. It is not enough just to sell many candles; you must make a profit on each sale. Figure out the precise cost of materials and the amount of time you spend, then make allowances for your experience. Be generous with your profit markup and stick to your price, but don't price yourself off the market. Consider your community's affluence and fix the price accordingly. Also try not to leave your candles on consignment. If they are not sold immediately, they will become shopworn from handling and you'll be the loser.

The unique forms, designs and combinations of color you will create with candles will be a fulfilling experience and may become rewarding financially as well. Thomas Edison, the man whose genius illuminated the world, once said, "I never did a day's work in my life. It was all fun." You are not Edison, you may say, but you too can light up the world—yours—and have fun doing it.

PART I

Making the Basic Candle

·Your Workshop·

Candlemaking is sculpture in wax. If you are to make this your medium of expression, you must master its techniques and then concentrate on creativity.

SETTING UP SHOP

You can set up a work area inexpensively and efficiently in your own kitchen with some help from the local five-and-ten-cent store.

To prepare your studio, wherever it may be, considerations must be given to work surface, tools and work clothes.

The area doesn't have to be large, but it should be clean and un-cluttered. The worktable must be level, otherwise the finished candle might tend to lean.

Because of the special characteristics of wax you must have access to water and heat. If you are fortunate enough to have a basement with running water and cooking facilities, that would be perfect. A corner in your garage with a portable stove and a handy garden hose is good, too. Wherever you work, do not pour melted wax into the sink. It will clog the pipes when it hardens.

PORTABLE STUDIO

But if you live in a city apartment, the kitchen can readily be made into a "portable studio." After each candlemaking session you can transfer your workshop into two cartons—your tools in one, your candlemaking materials in another—and stow them away in a closet or spare room.

To prepare for working, cover your work area with a layer of brown or wax paper. A large foil-covered cookie sheet would also do. I use aluminum foil most of the time because it molds itself to any surface and does not slide.

Do not use newspaper. The ink becomes imbedded in the wax drippings that accumulate during the pouring. Save these drippings; you will find use for them later. One of the delights of working with wax is that you can always melt down your failures and try again.

The stove on which you melt your wax should be carefully covered with tinfoil around the well of the burner you plan to use. Keep it free of wax to avoid the possibility of wax catching on fire. After covering your work surface you might spread out brown paper or an old plastic shower curtain or tablecloth to protect the floor.

CANDLEMAKING MATERIALS

Your materials include wax, wicks, stearic acid, magic crystals, color, scent and decorations. They will be described in greater detail in subsequent chapters.

TOOLS

Since the revived interest in candlemaking is comparatively recent, few specifically designed tools have appeared on the market, but you do not need them. Most of the tools you will come to depend on are part of any household. You can purchase the few extras you need in the local five-and-ten or hardware store.

At the beginning, assemble just a few pieces of rudimentary equipment: a hammer to break your slab of wax into small, usable pieces; a pair of pliers or scissors to cut your wicks; and a candy or candle thermometer to record the temperature of the heating waxes. You can melt wax down in a double boiler, or directly over the fire if you stand by the stove while you're heating it.

You will find yourself improvising other tools you may need as you go along. Several creative candlemakers I know use vastly different types of tools to achieve their very distinctive effects. A friend whose husband is a dentist decided to turn one of his discarded dental picks into her favorite candlemaking tool. You may think of something better, something no one has ever thought of before, to give your finished work just the right touch.

As a guideline, here is a list of items that I have come to depend on through the years:

Aluminum foil
Brown paper
Cake pans, two sizes
Cookie sheets and serving trays
Gloves
Hammer
Hot plate
Ice pick or knitting needle
Knife and linoleum cutter
Masking tape
Measuring spoons
Metal meat baster
Mold sealer
Mold weight

Molds
Pillowcase
Plastic bags
Pliers
Pot or double boiler
Potholder
Straight-edge ruler
Salad or vegetable oil
Scissors
Screwdriver
Silicone spray
Thermometer
Wastepaper basket or large
    container for water bath

Keep a list of your tools and materials. Before you settle down to work, spread out what you will need for a particular candlemaking operation. Have a special place for each item and always keep your supply of wax in a cool place and well covered.

KEEP TOOLS CLEAN

Anyone who works with tools knows that they perform with maximum efficiency only if they are cared for. Candlemaking equipment should be kept clean and free of wax and dust. When you've finished working take a few minutes to remove all the remaining wax from your tools, clean them thoroughly and put them back where they belong.

You're too tired, you say, to start cleaning equipment? There's no doubt that you are. But the leftover wax from today's project may ruin the bright promise of tomorrow's masterpiece.

WORK CLOTHES

Since you will be literally elbow deep in wax, it is a good idea to wear old clothing such as a smock, or better still, a plastic apron.

If you spill hot wax on your clothing, and you probably will, don't remove it immediately. It will be easier to peel off when it has solidified. For stubborn wax stains, place the fabric between two pieces of brown paper and press with a moderately warm iron. Usually the paper will absorb the stain. However, if the stain persists, dilute a cup of denatured alcohol in two cups of water and sponge the fabric clean.

· Wax ·

PARAFFIN

Though candles were used for centuries, little attention was given to their improvement. In the middle of the nineteenth century it was discovered that petroleum, used since historic times in magic and medicine, yielded a waxy substance which, when refined, became colorless, odorless and translucent. This is paraffin.

Its discovery offered advantages to the candlemaker, but it was not yet the perfect material. It was soft, burned too rapidly and dripped excessively.

STEARIC ACID

It was subsequently discovered that when paraffin was mixed with stearic acid, a substance derived from animal and plant life, its quality improved. The stearic acid made it harder, more opaque and longer-burning. This magical substance also gave the candle a smoother finish and added brilliance to the color.

The amount of stearic acid to add to paraffin depends on the melting point of the wax used and the type of candle one wishes to make. The higher the melting point of the wax, the less stearic acid is required, while more should be added to a lower-melting-point or softer wax. A dependable formula is three to four tablespoons of stearic acid to a pound of wax. For greater translucency, reduce the stearic acid; to increase opacity, add more. Mix in your stearic acid *after* the wax is completely melted.

MAGIC CRYSTALS

There is yet another wax additive called magic or luster crystals, known to the trade simply as "crystals." Crystals produce a hard, opaque, glasslike finish and improve the burning quality of wax. Having a high melting point, they must be dissolved separately in a small quantity of melted wax over an open flame to 212 degrees and blended in with the rest of the heated wax.

One to two teaspoons of magic crystals to a pound of wax is usually sufficient, but it is advisable to increase the quantities of both stearic acid and magic crystals in hot weather to give a better-burning quality to candles and to prevent their softening in the summer heat.

OTHER WAXES USED IN CANDLEMAKING

Beeswax, a substance secreted by honeybees, is a highly desirable, long-burning, aromatic but expensive wax.

Wax myrtle, known as bayberry or candleberry, is a shrub or tree with aromatic foliage and wax-coated berries which yield a substance used in candlemaking.

MELTING POINTS AND POURING
TEMPERATURES OF WAX

The melting point of wax is the temperature at which it changes from a solid to a liquid state, while its pouring temperature indicates the heat at which wax should be poured into the mold.

The melting points of wax for candlemaking range from 125 to 165 degrees and are classified as follows: low or soft (125–135 degrees); medium (143–150 degrees); high or hard (160–165 degrees). The melting points of wax vary with each manufacturer, though seldom more than 5 degrees.

The pouring temperature of a candle is determined by the type of wax, type of candle and the material of which the mold is constructed. It is best to pour wax at the highest temperature possible, for a hot wax produces a harder, longer-burning candle with a hotter flame and a minimum number of air bubbles. This, however, isn't always feasible. A glass container, for example, will shatter if filled with too hot a wax; while a plastic mold will become misshapen or melt. A hurricane candle, on the other hand, requires a high-temperature wax because it must withstand intense heat, otherwise the surrounding walls will melt.

The following table indicates the melting points and pouring temperatures of wax:

Type of mold	Type of wax	Melting point of wax	Pouring temperature
Cardboard	low	125–135 degrees	150–165 degrees
Glass	low	125–135 degrees	150–165 degrees
Plastic	low	125–135 degrees	150–165 degrees
Rubber	low	125–135 degrees	150–165 degrees
Plaster	medium	143–150 degrees	175–185 degrees
Hurricane	high	160–165 degrees	190–200 degrees
Metal	high	160–165 degrees	190–200 degrees
Sand*	high	160–165 degrees	165 or 275 degrees

* The pouring temperature of a sand candle depends on the effect you want to achieve. For a thin-crust sand pour at 165 degrees; for a thick crust, pour at 275.

Turn to your supplier for advice at the beginning. After working with candlemaking materials for a while, you'll soon get to know what best suits your particular needs.

HOW TO BUY WAX

Do not buy wax for candlemaking in your grocery store. What is good for jelly-making is not good for candlemaking. Check with your classified directory under "Oil Dealers" or locate a knowledgeable arts-and-crafts dealer and buy from him.

Don't overpay. Ordering from a faraway source may seem economical, but frequently the cost of shipping makes it more expensive in the long run. Inquire, compare, but don't sacrifice quality for price.

Wax comes in slabs of ten or eleven pounds, six to eight slabs in a carton. A carton may sound like a great deal of wax, but one block candle might consume six or more pounds.

It is even more thrifty to buy in larger quantities, and you might arrange to buy cooperatively with other candlemakers in your area. Moreover, it is a good idea to get to know candlemakers in the neighborhood in order to exchange ideas and share problems. You might even start a "candle clinic" to create community awareness of your group's efforts and insure a market, should you decide to go professional.

·Wicks ·

The beauty of candlelight, with its soft gentle glow, depends on the wick. Let's become acquainted with the wick, the heart of the candle, and get to know its characteristics, temperament and performance.

In bygone days wicks were crudely fashioned and made of ordinary string or cord. Today's wicks are scientifically designed of especially treated cotton material and come in a variety of shapes and sizes. The square-braided, flat-braided and metal-core wicks are most popular.

The flat-braided wick is used for candles under two inches in diameter.

The square-braided wick is for candles two inches in diameter and larger.

The metal-core wick comes in three sizes and has a lead wire running through its center, which melts away as the candle burns.

The three sizes are: *small,* used in container and general-utility candles under two inches in diameter; *large,* used in container and general-utility candles two to four inches in diameter; *extra large,* used in all types of candles four inches in diameter and larger.

HOW TO SELECT A WICK

The choice of wick is determined by the type of wax used and the diameter of the candle. A soft, fast-burning wax such as pure paraffin, for example, requires a thinner wick. Beeswax, hard and slow-burning, performs best with a thick wick.

To determine the correct wick size, measure the diameter of your candle mold both on the top and on the bottom, add the two and divide the sum in half. If the top is three inches and the bottom is five, you need a wick for a four-inch candle. You may use either the square-braided wick or the extra-large metal-core wick. Most mold manufac-

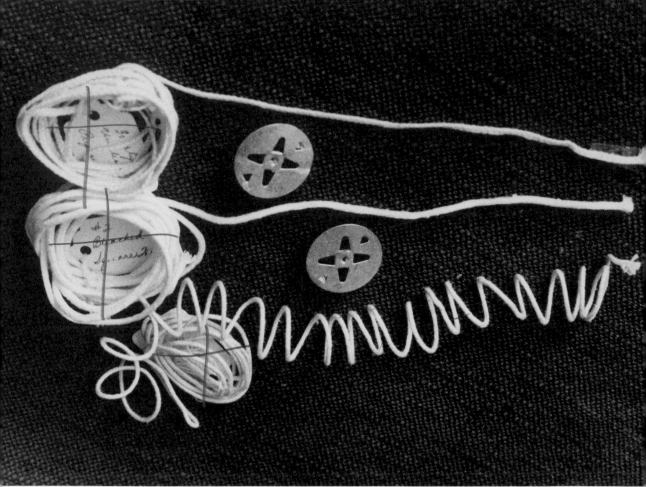

Wicks and wick tabs. MAD BOB RULES

turers today include wick information with their molds.

If a wick is too small for the diameter of the candle, the candle will drip and the wick will eventually sink into the melted wax, extinguishing the flame. On the other hand, if the wick is too large, it will smoke pitifully as if begging for a breath of air and throw off soot, too.

HOW TO MAKE A WICK

I don't recommend making your own wick, but if you are called upon to make a candle that requires an especially thick wick and you don't have one, cut lengths of thin wicking and braid the sections together. If you have no ready wicking at all, soak cotton yarn ten to twelve hours in a solution of one tablespoon of salt and two tablespoons of boric acid in a cup of water. Dry and braid it.

· Molds ·

"We know about heaven and the angels," it has been said. "Let's explore the way to get there."

Now that you are familiar with the special character of wax and wicks, let's explore how candles are made. Some are dipped, rolled or sculptured, but you will need molds for all others.

THEIR VARIETY

There are many varieties of molds: cardboard, glass, metal, paper, plaster, plastic and rubber. Many of these forms can be found in your own kitchen. Plaster or rubber ones may be purchased or you can make them yourself. The "professional molds" must be bought. These are constructed of metal and come in many shapes and sizes: tall, short, fat, slim, diamond-shaped, pyramidal, hexagonal, square and round. You can have Plexiglas tubes cut to your specification or metal ones made to order by a competent tinsmith. But you can take any kitchen container with a pleasing form and with just a few deft touches of your own transform it into an unusual shape.

A specially prepared liquid rubber with step-by-step instructions is available for candle molds. Plaster molds may be bought at craft and ceramic supply houses, and of course you can make your own. Great skill and precision are required in making them, and the beginning candlemaker should postpone his own mold-making.

The possibilities for candle shapes and designs are limitless. I have even used coffee-jar covers to make an exciting candle of more colors than the rainbow.

SPECIAL TECHNIQUES

There is just one simple rule to observe when you select a mold:

Professional molds.

it must be able to withstand heat and the weight of the molten wax.

The milk carton

Milk and cottage-cheese cartons are perhaps the most familiar variety of molds, but they must be reinforced to reduce the risk of seam-splitting and to avoid a pregnant look in the finished candle. Reinforce the top, center and bottom of paper containers with strong tape. For larger sizes—the half- or full-gallon milk carton—have boards cut to fit the sides. This is a one-time investment and a lifetime convenience. Place these boards around the carton and tape or tie string around them.

The round candle mold

The round candle mold is another familiar type. To make one, take a salad bowl or cut a rubber ball in half. Lubricate and fill the two halves with heated wax. When cool, fuse the surfaces by pouring hot wax on each and pressing the two together. When the wax is cool, pierce a hole through the center with a heated knitting needle. Tie a knot at one end of a metal-core wick or attach it to a metal tab, and insert the wick from the bottom.

When the candle is set, immerse it in a wax/water bath (explained on page 47) to give it a shiny finish. Apply metallic tape or other decorations to cover where the two halves were joined.

Improvising

Turn a paper cup upside-down and you have the makings of a tree; place one wax-poured Jello mold atop another and you have a stacked candle. If you want an especially tall candle, remove the bottom from all but the last of several large tin cans. Make sure there are no rims on the inside edges or you won't be able to remove the candle. Have a tinsmith solder them together or do it yourself, and the result will be a nonleaning Tower of Pisa.

CARE OF THE MOLD

Molds are your very special tools. Protect them by cleaning them thoroughly after each pouring, and keep them dry to avoid rusting. Don't put metal molds in the oven at a temperature higher than 175 degrees or the solder will melt. Don't strike your molds, and never

Homemade molds.

use steel wool or coarse abrasives to clean them. The slightest scratch or dent in the metal will reproduce a flaw in the candle.

If wax accumulates inside your metal mold because you have neglected to clean it, place it on an aluminum-foil or cookie sheet in your oven for fifteen minutes at 175 degrees and the wax will melt away. Then wash and dry the mold and store it in a plastic bag to keep it dust-free.

· Color ·

Especially prepared dyes for candlemaking are available in liquid, powder or solid form. You can make your own by mixing concentrated dyes with wax, but this is time-consuming and the results aren't always uniform.

The professionally prepared dyes assure an even coloring throughout. If you use pellets, as many candlemakers do, shave off a small portion and swish it through the melted wax to achieve the shade you want.

The art of coloring candles seems fraught with don'ts rather than dos. Don't use water-soluble dyes such as those used for food or cake coloring. Never use crayons; the preservatives in crayons cause the candle flame to sputter and smoke exasperatingly, and often to "go out like a light." Furthermore, crayon coloring leaves the candle

Color pellets.

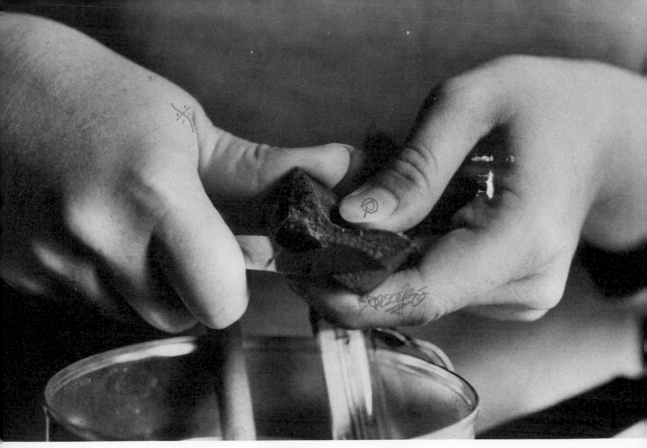

To assure even coloring, shave off small portions of the color pellet.

muddy and dull instead of vibrant. Lipstick also does not blend easily with wax, though some candlemakers insist on using it.

There are those who claim to use oil paints with excellent results. The two drawbacks are that oil paint doesn't mix readily and that it is frightfully expensive.

Use commercial colors especially prepared for candles. Stir them in *after* the wax is melted, and tend the pot while the dye is dissolving because scorched wax changes color.

Begin with a small amount of dye; add more gradually. Since it is impossible to judge color accurately by peering into the pot, a few drops of melted wax on a white saucer or in a bowl of cold water will give you an approximate idea of the tint. Keep in mind, though, that the color of the finished candle will be more intense than the small sample.

If you've put in too much dye, add clear melted wax to reduce the intensity. And if you're especially pleased with a color, make a note of the combination for future reference.

· Scent ·

A delicately colored candle, artistically decorated and appealingly scented, will add sheer delight to a dinner party or to a romantic supper for two.

Fragrances such as apple blossom or sandalwood enhance any occasion or decor. A sweet-scented candle will give a welcome fragrance to the atmosphere of a sickroom, and on a warm summer evening you can count on citronella to keep your patio free of those bothersome insects. The only restriction is your very own preference. Let it always be subtle.

All manner of provocative bouquets are available for candle-making in solid form or in liquid vials containing half an ounce to eight ounces of essence. Don't attempt to experiment with your favorite perfume, cologne or after-shaving lotion. You will be wasting the precious stuff and the equally valuable time you spent making your candle. An alcohol-base perfume is *not* compatible with wax. It will literally go up in smoke, while the fragrance of an oil base will linger on. Furthermore, a non-oil odorant will cause the wax to dull or form snow spots in the candle interior.

FORMULA

A little experimentation on your own will help establish a formula that most pleases you. A workable rule is a quarter ounce of undiluted scent stirred into two or three pounds of wax.

TECHNIQUES

You may apply scent in a variety of ways: soak the wick in it before securing it in the mold; pour the scent into the cavity of the candle

33

when refilling the well; or add a drop to the well each time you light the wick. I find it most effective to add the scent to my melted wax just before I pour the mold. *Don't pour the scent in after the mold is filled,* unless your aim is to achieve a mottled effect.

If you light more than one candle, avoid the use of conflicting scents in the same room. And whenever possible, place the candle in a low place, for fragrances rise and permeate the atmosphere.

If you notice after a while that the scent is too faint for your taste, rub the candle with a nylon stocking. It will restore the fragrance and bring a sheen to the surface of the candle as well.

With these few suggestions, a slab of wax, a touch of scent, a grain of imagination and a dash of good taste, you, in your own kitchen, can stir up an unforgettable ambrosia.

· Making the Candle ·

You have your wax and wicks. You are familiar with their characteristics and temperament and you are now ready to begin kitchen witchcraft in earnest. Use a double boiler, coffee pot or other heat-resistant vessel for melting your wax. If it has a spout, all the better, for melted wax is hard to control as you pour.

Put your slab of wax into an old pillowcase. Break it into small chunks with a hammer and place them in the pot, adding more as the wax melts. The smaller the chunks, the faster they will melt. For easier pouring, don't fill the pot to the top, and keep the outside free of wax. It may ignite.

If you use a double boiler, wipe the outside dry before you pour. Water and wax do not mix. Remember not to pour wax into the sink, for it will solidify as it runs down the drain and will cause the pipes to clog.

FIRE PRECAUTIONS

There are other precautions you should take at this point. In the event that your wax does catch fire, keep near the stove an open box of baking soda, salt or sand, an inexpensive fire extinguisher or a pot lid for smothering the flame. *Never use water to fight a wax fire.*

Precaution, of course, is the best prevention. Turn off the flame if there is any household distraction.

MELTING THE WAX

Heat your wax at least twenty degrees above its melting point, stirring frequently to keep an even temperature. Always keep a thermometer in the melting pot to insure the accuracy of the melting temperature.

It is important to remember that *wax does not boil*. When overheated, wax smokes, scorches and turns a dirty brown. Overheated colored wax makes the candle dull and lifeless instead of vibrant.

HOW MUCH WAX TO MELT

To make sure you're melting the right amount of wax for the size candle you want, place a sturdy plastic bag inside the mold and fill it with water. Pour the water into your wax-melting vessel and mark a level line on the outside to indicate the amount you need. Wipe the inside of the pot before you put in the wax. Keep adding chunks until the melted wax reaches that point. Add an extra cup or two, depending on the size of the mold, for refilling the wick cavity as the wax around it cools and contracts.

Keep a thermometer in the melting pot to make sure the temperature is constant.

PREPARING THE MOLD

While the wax is melting, prepare your mold for pouring. Make sure it is clean, dust-free and thoroughly dry. Lubricate your mold for easy removal of the candle. If you plan to wick the mold before pouring, lubricate it first and then thread it. Lubricate your metal mold with a parting agent known as silicone spray or a light vegetable or salad oil. Milk cartons have a waxy interior surface and don't really require lubrication, but I prefer to oil mine. Always wipe down excess lubricant or turn the mold over and let it drain off.

WICKING THE CANDLE

A candle may be wicked before pouring the wax or after it is removed from the mold. Professional molds come with wick holes and instructions for attaching the wick. For many homemade molds, you must pierce the hole yourself.

A metal-core wick may be used without making a hole in the bottom of the mold. To insert the metal-core wick, crimp one end and center it in the bottom of the mold. Secure it by pouring a small quantity of hot wax around it. Attach the other end to a bar placed across the top of the mold.

Warning!

Make sure the wick stands straight and is centered in the candle, but avoid exerting pressure. Stretching may make the wick too thin for the diameter of the candle, causing dripping and at times prompting the flame to drown in the heated wax.

Using the correct wick

Using the correct wick, properly centered in the mold, will assure even burning. If the wick is off center, the wax nearest the flame will melt more rapidly, leaving the opposite wall looking like an old ruin.

Wicking the milk carton

To wick the milk carton, use a metal-core wick or turn the mold over, locate the center on the bottom and pierce a hole with a sharp object from the outside inward. Cut the wick, allowing two inches on each end for tying and handling. Make a knot at one end and dip the other in hot wax for easy threading. When the wax has solidified, gently straighten the wax end between your fingers and push it through the wick hole until it comes out the top end of the mold. Place a pencil or bar across the top and tie the wick around it. Reinforce the bottom with tape or mold sealer to further secure against leakage.

Wicking the metal mold

The metal mold comes with a ready-made wick hole on the bottom. Simply dip one end of the wick in wax. Let it solidify, then thread it through the bottom, bringing it up to the top. Tie it to the wick holder. If no wick holder came with your mold or if you have misplaced it, put a pencil or bar across the top and tie the wick around it. Now turn the mold over again and secure the bottom with a retainer screw, winding the wick under it, counterclockwise. Reinforce the surrounding area with tape or mold sealer. Straighten and gently tighten the wick on top, and retie if necessary.

Wicking the tin can

To wick a tin can, pierce a hole in the bottom of the container from the outside or use a metal-core wick without making a hole. Insert the wick, using the same procedure you would use to wick a milk carton.

Wicking the finished candle

To wick the candle after it is out of the mold, pierce a hole through the center of the wax with a heated knitting needle, ice pick or hand drill. *Do not use an electric drill,* for it may melt too much wax around the hole. Moreover, applying too much pressure may cause the candle to crack. If you pierce too large a hole, refill it with hot wax *after* the wick is inserted.

Inserting the no-hole wick

There are molds which you cannot pierce a hole through, such as glass containers, Jello forms or bottles. For these molds use a metal-core wick. Tie one end to a button, dressmaker's weight or a commercial wick tab, and center it on the bottom of the mold. Tie the other end to a pencil or wick bar placed across the top of the mold.

Candles as wicks

Take a store-bought candle or make one yourself and use it as a wick. Press the candle into the center of the mold after the wax is poured and partially solidified.

Multiple wicks

Thread two or more wicks in a candle with a large diameter to achieve a novel effect and to gain more light, too. You may insert these wicks before pouring the wax or after the candle is removed from the mold.

WARMING THE MOLD

Lubricate the mold and thread the wick. Metal molds should be placed in a low-temperature oven, not above 175 degrees, and warmed for ten minutes. Heat plastic and glass molds on a radiator or electric pad, or place them in a container of hot water, making sure no water gets inside.

POURING THE MOLD

Bring the wax to its pouring temperature. As mentioned earlier, different types of candles and molds require waxes of different melting points and pouring temperatures. Pour wax at the highest tempera-

Dip the end of the wick in heated wax.

Thread the wick through the bottom of the mold.

Bring the wick through to the top and tie it.

Secure the wick on the bottom with a retainer screw.

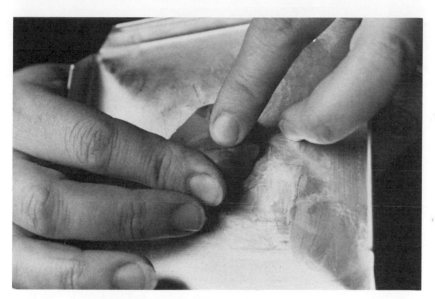

Reinforce the retainer screw with mold sealer.

Straighten and tighten the wick and retie it if necessary.

Pour wax down the side of the mold, not down the center.

ture for the particular mold you're using, for a hot wax produces a harder, longer-burning candle, minimizes air bubbles and adds greater vibrancy to the color.

Before pouring the mold make sure it is clean, dry, warm, well-lubricated and standing on a level surface. Tilt the mold, hold the pouring vessel close to it and direct the liquid against the wall, not the center of the mold, just as you would pour a glass of beer. This will further minimize the formation of bubbles.

Fill the mold to within three inches of the top and let it stand two or three minutes to give entrapped bubbles a chance to rise to the surface. You may rotate the mold gently or tap it slightly to break up any internal air pockets.

WATER BATH

The water bath is an indispensable step in the making of professional-looking candles. It makes it easier to remove the candle from the mold and gives a smooth finish to the candle surface.

Fill a container such as a large pail or wastebasket with lukewarm —not cold—water. Immerse the poured mold in it. Make sure the

Place a poured mold in a lukewarm water bath.

water reaches above the level of the wax but does not overflow into the mold. Don't add any water after the mold is placed in the bath, for the slightest change in temperature will leave a bubbly circle around the finished candle. Remove the mold from the bath after the last refilling of the wick area or when the candle is completely cooled.

The wax-filled mold may float and even tip over into the water bath. To avoid this, place a brick or an extra-large can of juice on top of the mold.

Place a brick on top of the mold to keep it from floating.

REFILLING THE WICK CAVITY

As the wax cools it contracts and a cavity or well forms around the wick area. Push a knitting needle or rod down the center to break up the outer crust and to relieve the inner tension, but watch that the hot wax doesn't squirt into your face.

Refill the well with the hot wax you've saved for this purpose. Two or three refillings may be necessary until a quarter-inch depression remains around the wick. Don't fill it to the very top, for wax may run over into the mold, causing the candle to stick and to be hard to remove.

COOLING THE CANDLE

Cool the candle at room temperature, away from any draft, for eight to twenty-four hours, depending on its size. Don't remove the candle from the mold until it is thoroughly set, or it will burn unevenly and too rapidly.

Candles should *never* be cooled at subzero temperature or in a deep-freeze. Extreme cold is a shock to wax and will cause cracking and affect the burning quality of the candle.

REMOVING THE CANDLE FROM THE MOLD

The Metal Mold

Untie the wick at the top, release the wick at the bottom and turn the mold over on a clean towel. The candle should slide out. If it doesn't, try pulling it out by its wick. If it still resists, place the candle in the refrigerator, *not the freezing compartment,* for ten to fifteen minutes, turning the mold around a few times to assure even cooling. Now try removing it. If it still doesn't come out easily, plunge the mold in hot water for a few seconds and roll it on a flat surface as you would a rolling pin. It should come out.

Don't use any sharp instruments to release the candle; they will scratch the mold and mar the candle surface as well.

The Milk Carton

Gently knead the sides of the carton until the candle is released, or strip the carton away.

The Glass Mold

Submerge the mold in hot water and plunge it into an ice-cold bath. The glass should break. You may also reverse the procedure and put the mold in the refrigerator until it feels cold to the touch, then plunge it in hot water. This is a less desirable method, for the cold may cause the candle to emerge with a fractured appearance.

Another alternative is to break the container. Use a glass cutter or wrap the mold in a plastic or paper bag and tap it with a hammer until the glass shatters.

Removing a candle from a metal mold.

FINISHING THE CANDLE SURFACE

After the candle is removed from the mold, examine it carefully for imperfections. Scrape seam lines with a dull-edged knife; and for that apple-shine look, polish it with a nylon stocking or a cloth pre-treated for shining cars. You may also use a clear candle spray or a clear shoe-polish spray.

THE WAX/WATER BATH

The wax/water bath is another way of finishing your candle. I dip my candles in a high-melting wax heated to 240 degrees, in a vessel deep enough to cover the candle completely. If you plan to do it, protect your hands and wrists against the hot wax with a pair of old cotton gloves. Hold the candle by its wick with a pair of pliers or your fingers and lower it into the vessel. Count to five and quickly withdraw the candle, then submerge it in a pail of ice water. Remove and let the candle stand until it is thoroughly dry, then submerge it again in hot wax—always concluding with the ice-cold bath.

Colored wax/water bath

To add variety or restore color to a woefully faded candle, dip it into a tinted wax/water bath at 190 to 200 degrees, no higher, to protect the surface from softening or melting.

LEVELING THE CANDLE

Level the bottom of the candle by rotating it on a heated surface such as an electric hot plate or a warm skillet.

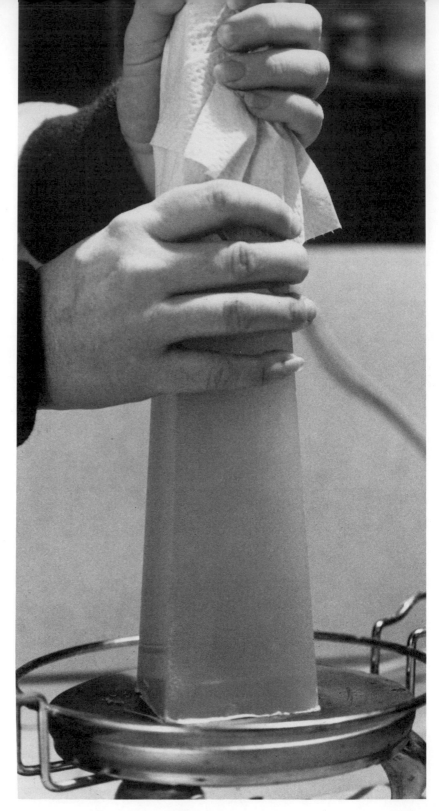

Level the bottom of the candle on a hot plate.

LAST-MINUTE HINTS

Handle a candle by its wick *only*; never touch its surface. The oil in your skin will leave fingermarks.

Postpone trimming the wick if you plan to decorate your candles. That extra length of wick makes the candle easier to handle when you are dipping or decorating.

When you remove the candle from the mold, try inverting it to see if you might have created still another graceful line.

When the candle is complete, trim the wick tip to one-half inch.

· Basic Candlemaking Steps ·

Pierce a hole around the wick area with   page 44
a knitting needle or wire when
the wax forms a crust.

Refill the wick cavity two or more times   page 44
until a quarter-inch depression remains.

Allow the candle to set at room   page 44
temperature away from a draft.

Remove the candle from the mold.   page 45

If you did not insert the wick before   page 38
pouring, do so now.

Clean seams and remove surface imperfections.   page 47

Decorate your candle, if you wish.   page 56
(Also see Candle Gallery, page 63.)

Dip the candle in a wax/water bath   page 47
or use a spray finish.

Level the bottom of the candle.   page 47

Cut the wick to size.   page 49

·What Have I Done Wrong?·

Blemishes

Blemishes inside the candle are caused by too much scent in the wax; spots on the outside are caused by handling the candle with soiled hands. Rub softly with a nylon stocking to clean candle and redip in a wax/water bath for a shiny finish.

Blisters

Blisters or pimples are caused by storing candles in too warm a temperature. To clean, gently scrape off the blisters with the back of a knife or spatula, rub the candle with a nylon stocking and dip in a wax/water bath.

Brittleness

If a candle is brittle and crumbly, too much stearic acid and/or luster crystals have been mixed into the wax.

Bubbles

Bubbles appear around the candle if the water bath has not reached the wax level, or if more water was added after the mold was placed in the bath.

Bubbles are also caused by wax being poured down the center of the mold instead of against the sides, or by pouring from too great a height. After pouring the wax let the mold set two or three minutes to allow the air bubbles to rise to the top. You may help eliminate bubbles by gently rotating and tapping the mold.

Bulging

Candles bulge when they are made in molds not strong enough to withstand the weight of poured wax. Remove the bulges with a warm palette knife and dip the candle in a wax/water bath, or apply decorations to hide the flaws.

Cave-ins

If the well or cavity around the wick has not been refilled in time, the candle may collapse or cave in.

Chipping

Chipping is caused by using too much stearic acid or luster crystals, or by cooling the candle too quickly.

Cracks

Cracks may be caused by cooling the candle unevenly or refilling the wick area with a lower-temperature wax.

Dirt

Dirt can be removed by applying vegetable or baby oil with a soft cloth and polishing the candle gently with a nylon stocking.

Dripping

A candle drips because the wax is too soft or the wick is too small for the diameter of the candle. If it drips to one side, the candle is standing in a draft or the base is not level.

Dull finish

A dull finish results because the pouring temperature was too cold, the candle was cooled too slowly or too much scent was added. Overheated colored wax will also have a dull, lifeless finish.

Fractures

Fractures may appear inside the candle for several reasons. First, the water bath may have been cold rather than lukewarm. The candle itself may have been cooled in the refrigerator for too long a time, or in a deepfreeze. Finally, the wick cavity may have been refilled after the surrounding wax had cooled.

Frost marks

White streaks and frost-like blemishes appear inside the candle because the mold was too cold, the pouring wax was not hot enough, or because too much scent has been added to the wax, or has been poured into the mold without proper blending.

Holes

Holes appear because the mold was dusty or dirty, or because the wax was poured too fast.

Melted bottom

If a votive candle is placed inside a wax shell without its glass container or is left burning too long, it will melt the bottom of the candle mold.

Mottling

Mottling results for several reasons: The mold was too cold, the wax was poured too slowly, too much stearic acid and/or scent was added, the scent was added after the mold was filled, or the lubricating oil was left in the mold.

Pockmarks

Pockmarks appear when a candle has been poured at too high a temperature, too fast, or when it has cooled too slowly especially during hot, sultry summer days. Pockmarks may also appear when the wax is overheated, or when water seeps into the mold.

Sagging

If the sides of a hurricane or any other type of candle sag, it is made of too soft a wax, placed in too warm a room, has been burning too long or standing in a draft, or the votive is off center.

Smoking and sooting

A candle will smoke if the wick is too large for the diameter of the candle or the candle is standing in a draft.

Splashing

The wax will splash and sputter if the well around the wick has not been pierced and refilled.

Wax lumps

Lumps of unmelted wax will accumulate around the sides of a candle, especially if a high-temperature pouring wax is burned at short intervals.

White dots

White dots will appear in the candle if the mold was cold, if the wax was not hot enough when poured, if an alcohol-based fragrance was used to perfume the candle, or if the candle was removed from the mold before it was thoroughly set.

· Decorating the Candle ·

"To be creative," a wise man once said, "you must understand with your brain, see with your eyes and execute with your hands." This is applicable to all forms of art, including working with wax.

To make creative candles you need interesting shapes, designs, decorations, color, scent and most of all, imagination. Look into books on design in the library; visit art galleries and museums; study masterpieces, ancient and modern. All this is *art,* you may say. Indeed it is, but the creative principles are the same whether you work with paint, stone, wood or wax.

DECORATING TOOLS

The few tools needed for decorating candles are a hard work surface on which to prepare designs and cut decorations, a knife or linoleum cutter, geometric patterns, sheets of colored wax and an eggbeater or fork for whipping wax. You will also need a pair of scissors, screwdriver, palette knife, spatula, ruler, oil-soluble colors, brushes, glue, small straight pins, glitter and a large muffin tin for mixing and keeping colors warm.

You may think of other items for your own special designs, but to begin with these listed above will be sufficient, and most of them you already have. For more advanced decorating you might purchase an electric pen or a propane torch. Whatever you do, concentrate on creativity, not tools.

DECORATING SUGGESTIONS

The following are some suggestions to help you decorate your candles.

Tooling the candle surface with an electric pen.

Creating a design with a heated nail.

Cast or poured designs

Cast or poured designs are small wax decorations cast in plastic or metal molds. The molds can be purchased at craft shops. Apply these designs with heated straight pins, craft glue, or brush hot wax on both surfaces and press the decorations onto the candle.

Glass decorations

Arrange colorful pieces of glass into a design and attach them to a container with glue. You can also roll a glue-sprayed container in glass nuggets. Let the container dry, brush off the excess and place a votive candle in the center. You can also pour a block candle, arrange colorful pieces of glass on the outside and insert a votive candle in the center when the wick is partially burned down.

Glitter glue

Glitter glue is a combination of glue and glitter and comes in squeeze tubes or in spray cans. It is available in a variety of colors and is a valuable aid in decorating candles.

Applying glitter glue.

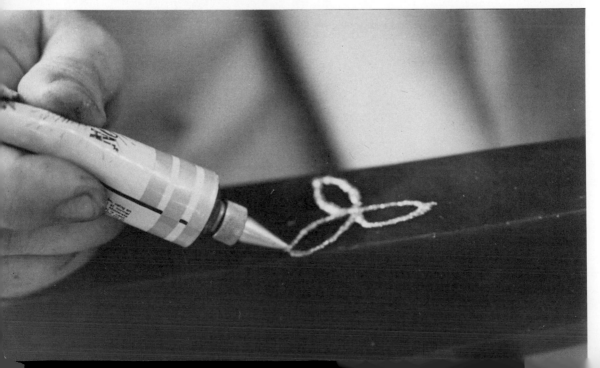

Jewelry

Bring out your "antiques"—those bits and pieces of jewelry you have neglected to throw away—and use them to add a novel touch to your candle. Attach jewelry with craft glue.

Lace designs

Dip lace in hot wax and attach it to the candle surface with craft glue. Do not immerse the candle in a wax/water bath; use a candle spray instead.

Metallic tape

This self-adhering tape comes in many colors and is available at craft shops.

Painted designs

Candles may be decorated by brushing or spraying paint on the candle surface. Crayons—the very ones that should not be used to color wax—may also be used. Heat the crayons first.

Rub'n Buff

Rub'n Buff is a brand name for a metallic paste that comes in a tube. It is available in a number of colors and is used for highlighting designs and decorations on candles.

Sheen

To add a luster to candles that cannot be submerged in a wax/water bath, apply a commercial spray made especially for finishing candles. This spray also protects the candle against fingermarks and scratches.

Wax sheets

Cut geometric designs—or any other shape you like!—from sheets of wax and attach them to your candles with craft glue, heated

Applying Rub'n Buff.

Cutting designs from wax sheets.

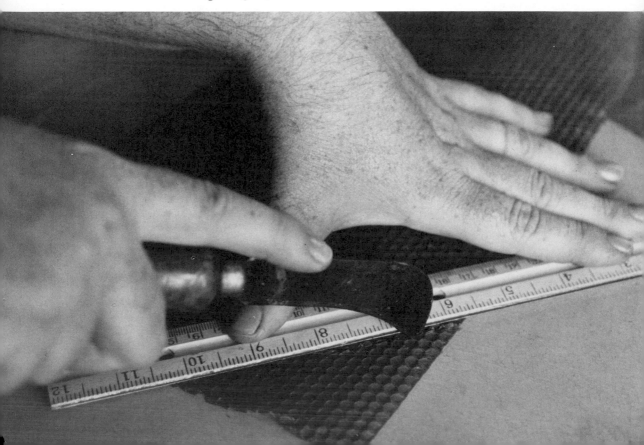

straight pins or hot wax. Do not dip these candles in a wax/water bath because the designs will fall off. Wax sheets are also used for making rolled candles. Directions for making rolled candles are on page 144.

Wax/water bath

Another way to add luster and even color to a candle is with the wax/water bath. Be sure that the vessel you use for the wax/water bath is larger than your tallest candle. The wax for dipping a newly made candle should be heated to 240 degrees. To "redo" or recolor a faded candle, dip it in melted wax at 190 degrees so that the original candle does not melt.

Whipped wax

Cool melted wax until a film forms on the surface and whip with a fork or an eggbeater to a fluffy consistency. Apply it to the candle, but work fast as the wax hardens quickly. Remelt and rewhip the wax when it solidifies.

There is a commercial whipped wax that comes in a cold liquid form that is easily beaten into a fluff and applied to the candle.

Whipping wax.

Applying whipped wax to a candle.

NOTE

To fireproof decorations: To prevent the burning of decorations imbedded inside or attached to the outside of a candle, remove them as the flame approaches. Dip decorations in sodium silicate, available at drugstores, to avoid their burning. They will char slightly, but they will not go up in flames.

PART II
Candle Gallery

To avoid repetition, basic candlemaking steps will not be included in the following pages unless they are necessary for clarity.

I. Fata Morgana

II. Mushroom candle

III. Sand candle with dye design

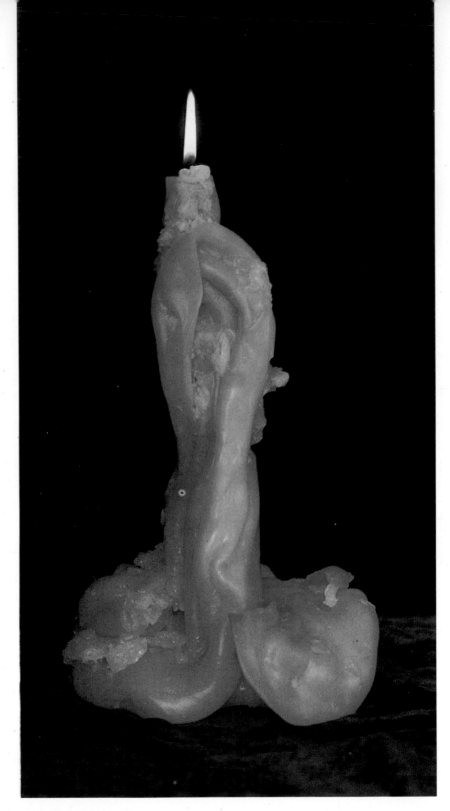

IV. Draped candle

V. Candy candle

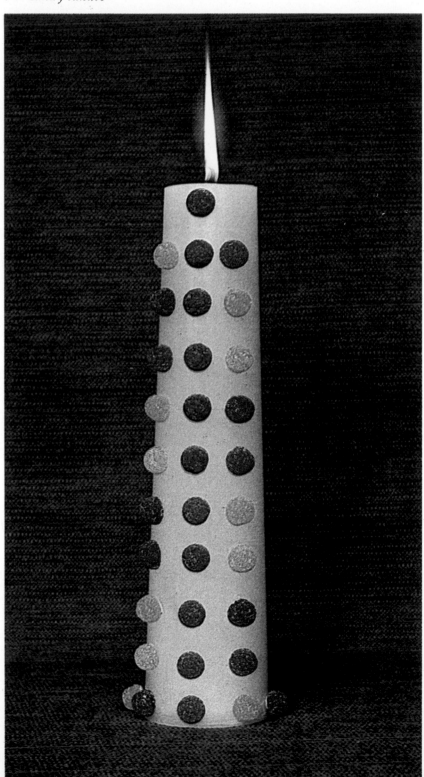

VI.
Carved candle

VII. Container candle

VIII. Rainbow candle

IX. Spear-tipped candle

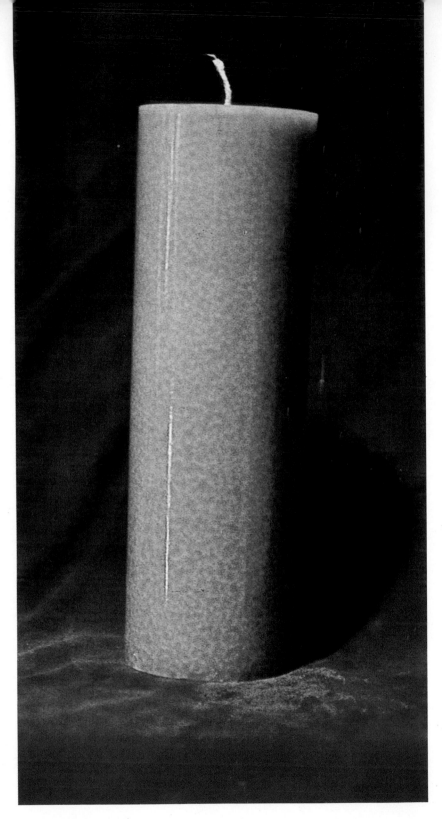

X. *Mottled candle*

XI. *Fried-marble candle*

XII. Rolled and cut candle

XIII. *Rolled candle*

XIV. *Stalagmite candle*

XV.
Appliqué candle

Abstract Design

Brush designs on the candle with colored wax, or use a heated
metal tool or electric pen to carve designs into the surface.

Carved Candle

Draw your own or copy a design on tracing paper. Outline the design on the candle surface with a blunt tool and carve it into the wax surface with a sharp instrument.

Melt away rough edges with a propane torch and apply metallic paste or Rub'n Buff to highlight the design.

Ciregraphic Candle

Ciregraphic refers to writing with wax. This is a candle decorated
by incising, carving or inscribing designs into its surface with
a heated tool.

Nailhead Design

Cut a pattern of the candle on paper to create your design. Keep a small container of colored wax over hot water or on a heating pad —not directly over the flame. Dip a broad nail or a small metal tool in the wax, and apply the decoration. Or, press a heated nailhead into the wax to achieve unusual effects and use Rub'n Buff to highlight the indentations. Do not use a wax/water bath; spray the candle.

Hammered Copper Candle

Pour a round or square candle and let cool. Using a heated tool, melt away areas on the surface to create the feeling of hammered copper. Or apply whipped wax on a molded candle and while the wax is still warm knead and press the surface to give the appearance of metal that has been hammered. When the wax is solidified apply Rub 'n Buff to emphasize the highlights.

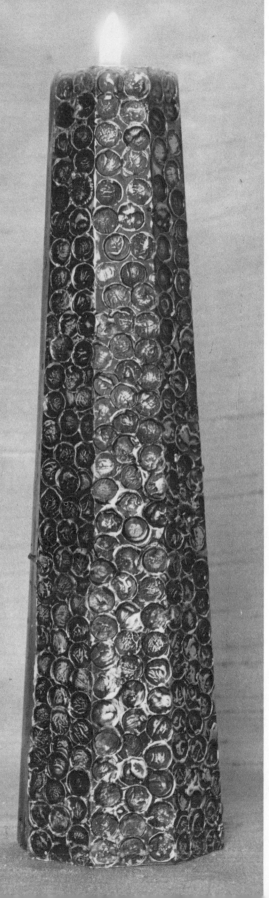

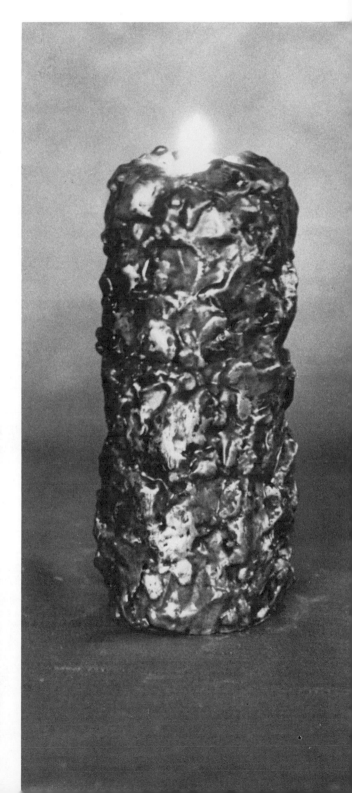

Appliqué

Appliqué means applied or laid on, as one material atop the other. In candlemaking, to appliqué is to place wax cutouts or molded designs on the surface of a candle. Use colored sheets of beeswax or molded decorations and attach them with glue or hot wax. Do not immerse the candle in a wax/water bath or the decorations may melt off. Give it a sheen spray instead.

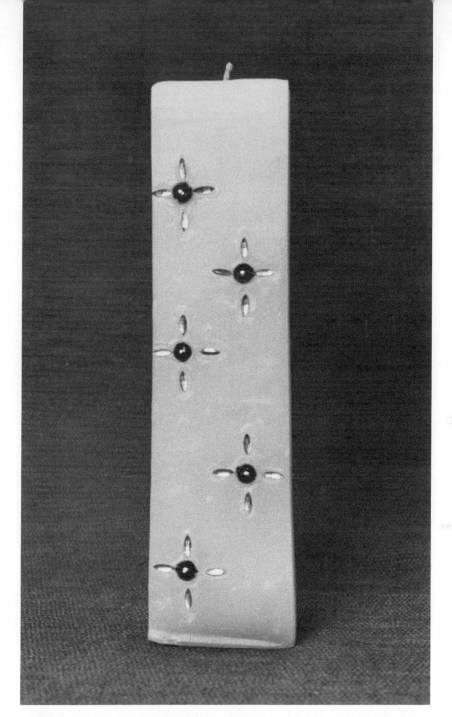

Beads and Jewels

Cut strips from a sheet of wax. Imbed bead or jewel designs into
the strips and attach them to the candle with hot wax or craft glue.
Also, try imbedding the beads or jewels directly in the candle by
heating and pressing them into the surface of the candle.

73

Branded Candle

Use a large, preferably square-shaped candle. Select a metal object such as a belt buckle or cookie cutter. Heat and press the object into the wax. When the wax cools, apply color to the "branded" area with a fine brush, or use Rub'n Buff to highlight the surface.

Candy Candle

To bring more fun to a child's party attach colorful candies or gumdrops to a candle. Either fit the candies into carved precut notches and attach them with heavy glue, or fasten them to the candle with heated straight pins.

Card Design

Cut decorative designs from Christmas or greeting cards or make your own. Place the design on the candle; cover with wax paper and press it into the surface with a warm iron or attach it with a craft glue. For a three-dimensional effect, build a whipped-wax frame around the design.

Leaves of Grass

Keep a library of ferns, leaves and stalks between sheets of aluminum foil or wax paper.

Arrange designs of leaves, flowers or grass on a candle. Cover with wax paper and press the decorations into the surface with a warm iron, or attach with craft glue.

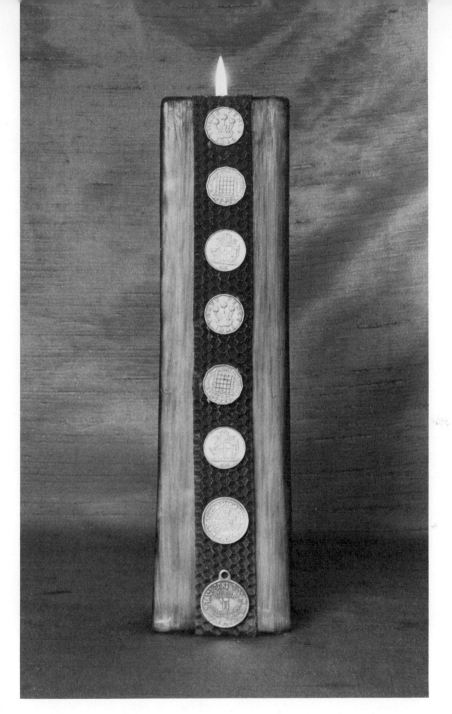

Medallion Candle

Press medals, foreign coins, colorful pieces of glass or other decorations into strips of home-poured or store-bought sheets of wax. Attach the strips to the candle with craft glue and weld the ribbon edges with a heated tool or electric pen.

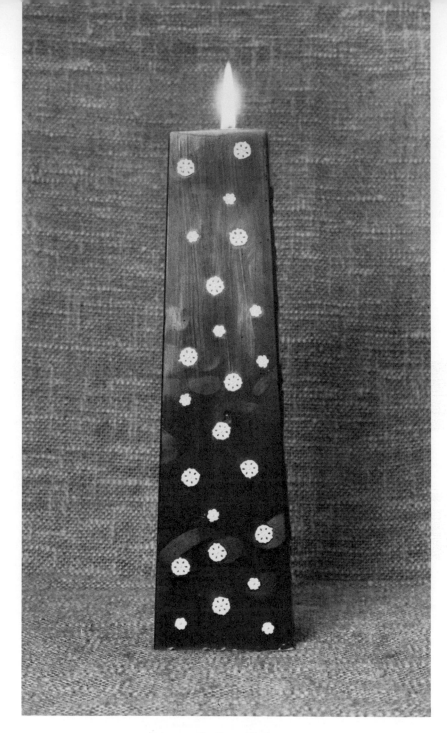

Snowflake Design

Buy snowflake designs or cut them out of doilies and attach them
with heated wax or craft glue to a dark-colored candle. Do not
use the wax/water bath. Spray the candle surface.

Mosaic Design

Arrange cubes of colored wax in a mosaic design and attach
them to the outside of the candle with a craft glue; or place the
cubes in the interior of the mold and fill it with a lower-temperature
wax than the cubes to prevent them from melting. Dip the candle
in a wax/water bath.

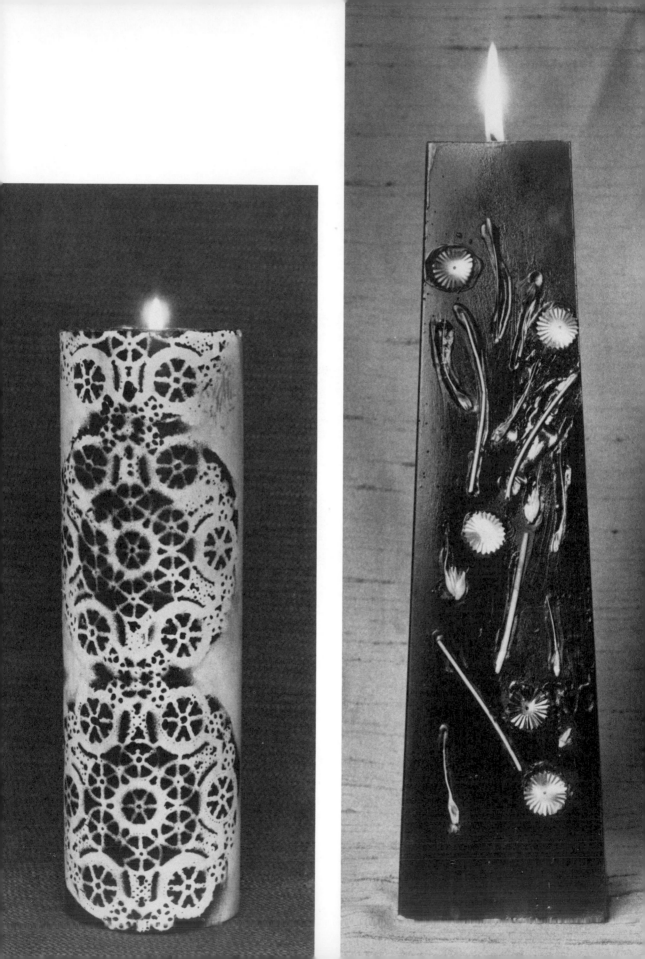

Doily Design

Wrap a doily around a tall cylindrical candle, secure it with Scotch tape and protect the surrounding surface with wax paper or aluminum foil. Brush or spray colored paint over the doily. The perforations will fill with color, leaving a design on the candle. Apply two or more coats to assure good coverage before removing the doily. Do not put the candle in a wax/water bath or the paint will come off.

Fireworks

Pour a large, deep-colored candle. Arrange a design of weeds or stalks on the candle to simulate a burst of fireworks. Cover the surface with wax paper and press the design into the candle with a warm iron. You may also arrange sequins to simulate a burst of fireworks.

Stained-glass Candle

Arrange pieces of stained glass in a pattern and attach them to the candle with craft glue or melted wax, or imbed them into the candle. Build a frame around the design with whipped wax. This is particularly effective in a hurricane candle. If the glass is not too dark, the light from inside the candle will create the illusion of glowing church windows on a snowy, wintry night.

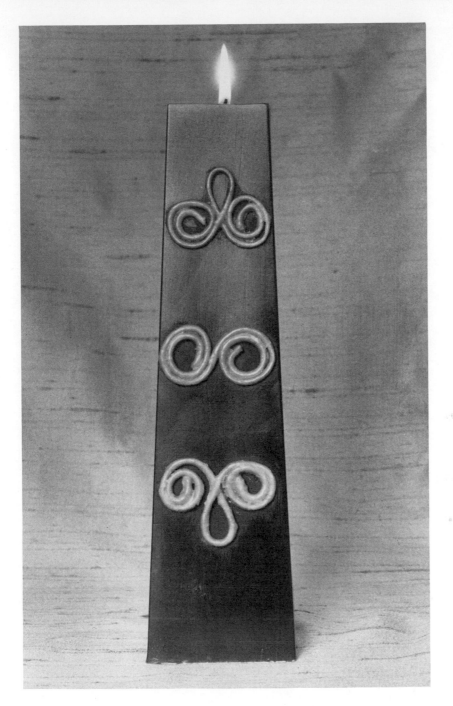

Spaghetti or Macaroni Design

Cook spaghetti, and when it is pliable, form it into interesting designs. Dip in hot colored wax and attach to the surface of a candle. Interesting patterns and designs may also be made with macaroni.

Candle-in-the-Pot

Decorate the outside of a clay flowerpot with gay designs. Plug
the drainage hole and pour a candle, or fill the pot with melted
wax and place a votive in the center.

Forever Candle

A candle provides light to others as it consumes itself. Here is an example of one you can burn and keep, too.

Center an inverted votive glass in the bottom of a mold and fill it with high-melting wax. When set, turn the mold over and put a votive in the glass, replacing it when it burns out.

Suggestion: Thread and pour a mold. When the candle is burned down sufficiently to accommodate a votive glass, press one into the center.

Container Candle

A container candle is burned in the receptable into which it is poured. For a translucent candle in a glass container, do not add stearic acid to the wax, and pour at a low temperature or the container will break. Container candles may be decorated with beads, sequins, decals or stencils, or designs may be painted on the outside.

Snowball

Use a professional mold or cut a rubber ball in half. Pour a candle. Dip it in whipped wax and arrange clusters of holly leaves and berries into the surface.

Dinner Candles

Dinner candles are long, thin tapers and usually provide a formal effect. Their name comes from the fact that they are the type of candles used on a dinner table. Directions for making dinner candles are on page 136.

Fried-marble Candle

Place a votive candle in a brandy snifter and surround it with
fried colored marbles or chunks of stained glass. The lit votive
will highlight the shiny glass balls or chunks, giving off an alluring
glow.

Hanging Candle

Buy a sling or make one of suede, plastic or smooth leather.
Enclose a large candle in it, but make sure there is sufficient
clearance between the flame and the sling.

Floating Candles

For an unusual effect, pour hot wax into small, individual Jello molds or jar covers. When the wax is partially cooled insert a metal-core wick or small birthday candle in each form. Let set. Remove from the mold and float candles in a dish of water.

Suitable fragrances added to the wax and gaily colored flowers scattered on the water add yet another dimension to the blaze of light.

Hurricane Candle

This popular design is patterned after the hurricane lamp. The difference is that the lamp flame is enclosed in glass, while the candle is surrounded by a wax exterior.

Pour a high-melting wax at 190–200 degrees. Do not add stearic acid or luster crystals, for you want the walls to be translucent. When a quarter-inch shell forms around the interior, break the top crust and pour out the excess. Level the inside walls and top edges.

If the shell is too massive, repour hot wax and swish it around until the walls melt down to the desired thickness. Invert the mold, allowing the excess wax to drain off, leaving the walls even. Attach decorations to the inside or the outside or incise carved designs on the mold and place a votive in the center.

Keep the burning candle away from drafts to prevent the wall nearest the flame from melting away. Also, the hurricane candle shouldn't be burned more than two-and-a-half to three hours at one time or the shell will begin to soften and sag.

Nutshell or Seashell Candles

Secure a metal-core wick or a small birthday candle in a seashell or nutshell. Fill the shells with hot wax. When a number of them have set, arrange them in a shallow, water-filled dish to add a festive glow to a special occasion.

Grapefruit or Melon Candles

Scoop out the inside of half a grapefruit or melon and fill it with hot wax. When the candle is set, cut away the rim and insert a metal-core wick. Or place a votive in the mold before pouring the candle.

Corrugated Candle

For an interestingly textured candle, measure corrugated cardboard to fit the inside of a milk container, preferably a half-gallon or larger. Align the seam of the corrugated cardboard, secure it with masking tape and place it in the container. Thread the wick, lubricate and pour the mold. When the wax is set, strip the carton away and dip the candle in a wax/water bath.

Suggestion: Try using wide cardboard mailing tubes.

Sand Candles

Fill a dish or box with damp, *not* wet, sand. Scoop out the
center. For legs make three half-inch indentations in the sand with
a dowel or your fingers. Fill the mold with hot wax. If the
diameter is large insert two or more wicks.

For a *thick crust* use drier sand and pour wax at 270–280 degrees;
for a *thin crust* pour the wax in wetter sand at 165 degrees.

When the wax is partially set you may wish to splatter the
surface with powdered or liquid color, or scatter colorful chunks
on top. For crumbly-shaped candles, press aluminum foil in a dish,
combine pebbles or seashells with sand and pour your wax.

Twisted, Braided or Rope Candles

A twisted, braided or rope candle can be made by imbedding a wick into a wide strip of wax and shaping it into a winding, braided or rope form. But you stand the risk of getting the wick off center, causing the candle to burn unevenly and drip heavily.

However, molds are now available for casting these intricate-looking candles. Simply select the shape you wish and follow the instructions for pouring.

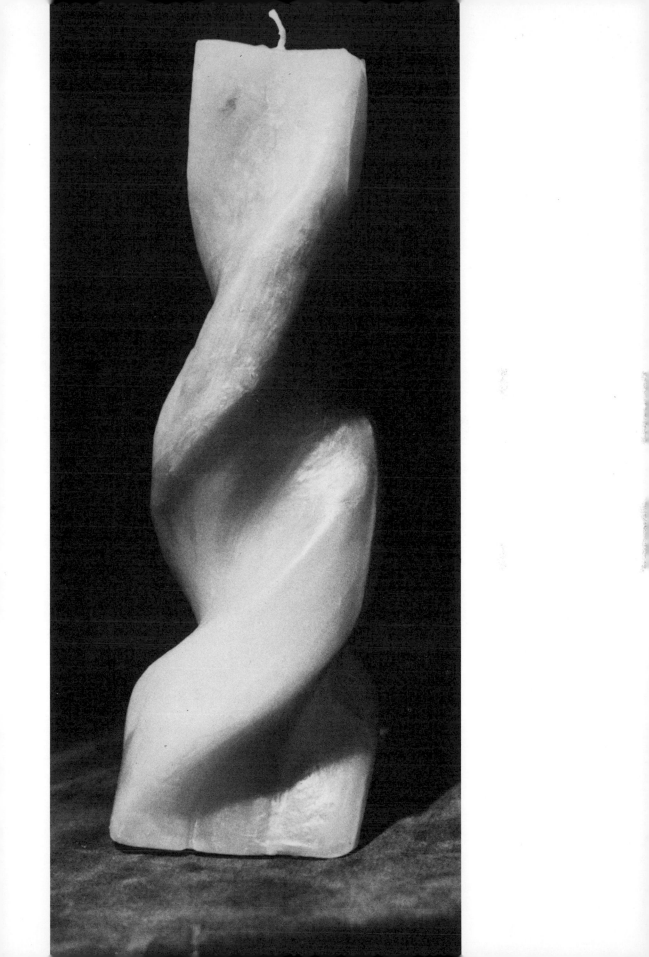

Wrapped Candles

Wrapped candles are made by pouring wax into a flat rubber design mold and then wrapping the wax design around a blank candle. Detailed instructions for making a wrapped candle are on page 147.

Cactus Candle

Cut three or more strips of different lengths from sheets of poured wax. Place a wick in the center of each and roll into tubular shapes. With additional pliable wax, knead and form them into a unit with a base. Dip the candle into a wax/water bath.

Flowers

Fresh, artificial or wax-sculptured flowers may be used to make flower decorations for candles.

Immerse *fresh petals,* one at a time, into hot *colored* wax and submerge quickly in ice water. Dry them thoroughly before immersing them again. Dip until desired thickness is achieved. Immerse *artificial flower petals* and *leaves* two or three times in *clear,* melted wax to give them body.

To make your *own* flowers, pour melted wax onto lukewarm water or onto an oiled cookie sheet. Cut and bend the wax into leaf and petal shapes, or use cardboard patterns and trace them on sheets of wax. Keep two pans of water handy; one hot, to make the wax cutouts pliable, the other cold, to harden them. Mold and form the leaves and petals to the desired flower shapes.

To add a bit of realism, notch or serrate the leaves with a pin, a small blade or pinking shears. Etch veins in larger leaves with a darning needle.

To attach the flowers to a candle, use a heated spatula or small spoon. Scrape the sides of the candle and apply hot wax to the scraped area and to the backs of the flowers. Firmly press the decorations into the surface. You may also apply flowers with a strong glue.

Foliating Candle

Pour heated wax in a large mold and add a commercial foliating compound, as directed. Burn the candle from three to four hours continuously, or until the flame softens the walls of the candle. Pour out the accumulated melted wax from the well. Applying pressure, form the soft shell into designs resembling curling leaves or the shape of a ram's horn.

Free Form

Line a deep bowl with crushed aluminum foil. Fill with clear or
colored wax, and when the wax is cool yet malleable, remove it from
the bowl and shape it with your hands into unusual forms. Wick
and submerge the candle in a wax/water bath, or give it a spray
sheen.

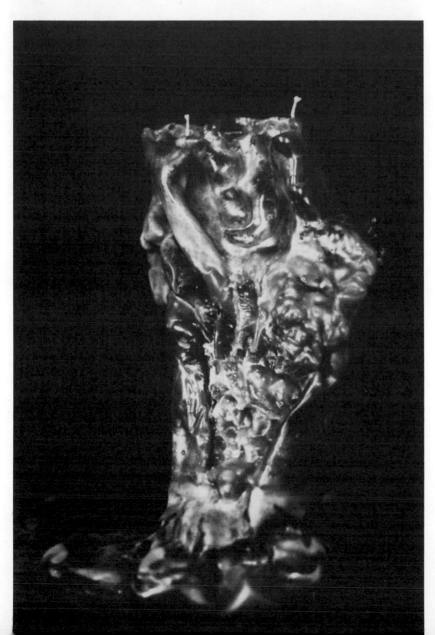

Fata Morgana

Because of its unreal, illusory appearance I call this candle Fata
Morgana. It is simple to make and unpredictable in result; no two
Fata Morganas ever look alike.

Secure a blank candle in a bowl with half a cup of hot wax and
let cool, or make your own blank by shaping a lump of warm wax
into a free form, placing a wick in its center. Wearing long sleeves
and using gloves to protect your hands and arms, pour two ounces of
wax at 165 degrees in a pail of lukewarm water. Do not add
stearic acid or luster crystals to the wax or the candle will be too
brittle, and make sure the water is deep enough to submerge the
entire blank candle and bowl. Set the wax-topped water in motion
and slowly immerse the blank candle in the liquid. Give it a few
swirls and then remove it. A Fata Morgana!

Stalagmite Candle

Lubricate the outside of a tall vessel or bottle and invert it on a cookie sheet or tinfoil. Melt high-temperature colored wax, and when a film appears on the surface, pour or drip it slowly over the vessel until the desired effect and thickness are achieved. Cool. If the shell is difficult to remove from the vessel, turn the vessel over and fill it with warm water. The shell should loosen and slide off in a few seconds. Insert a votive candle in the center.

Suggestion: Apply two or more colors alternately.

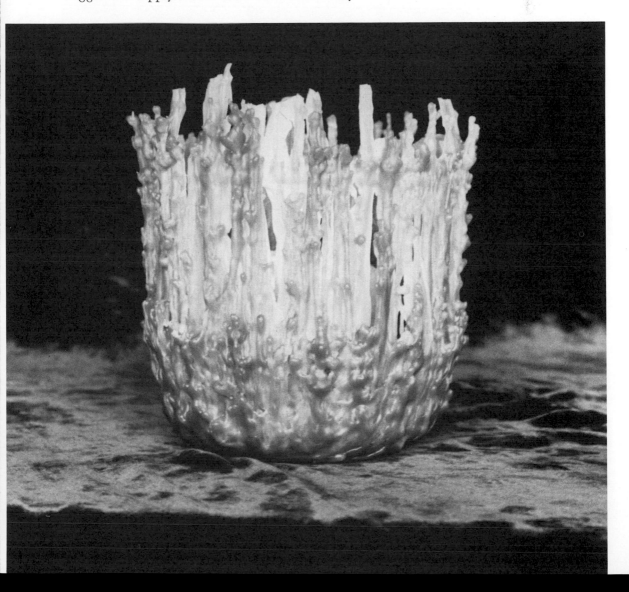

Mushroom Candle

Soften a piece of wax and knead it with your hands into a stemlike shape. For the top or head of the mushroom, fill a bowl with melted wax. When the wax is cool, attach the top to the kneaded stem with craft glue. Insert a wick and plunge the candle into a wax/water bath. Dribble wax or etch a design on top of the mushroom with a heated tool, if you wish.

Suggestion: Make a depression in sand with a bowl for the head. Imbed a narrow-necked bottle for the stem. Pour wax in each cavity, and when it has set, attach the two parts. Thread the wick and immerse in a wax/water bath.

Dipped Candles

Dipped candles are made by dipping wicks repeatedly in melted wax, slowly letting the wax accumulate until the candles are the size you want. Although it is not necessary, you usually make a number of dipped candles at the same time. Detailed instructions are on page 137.

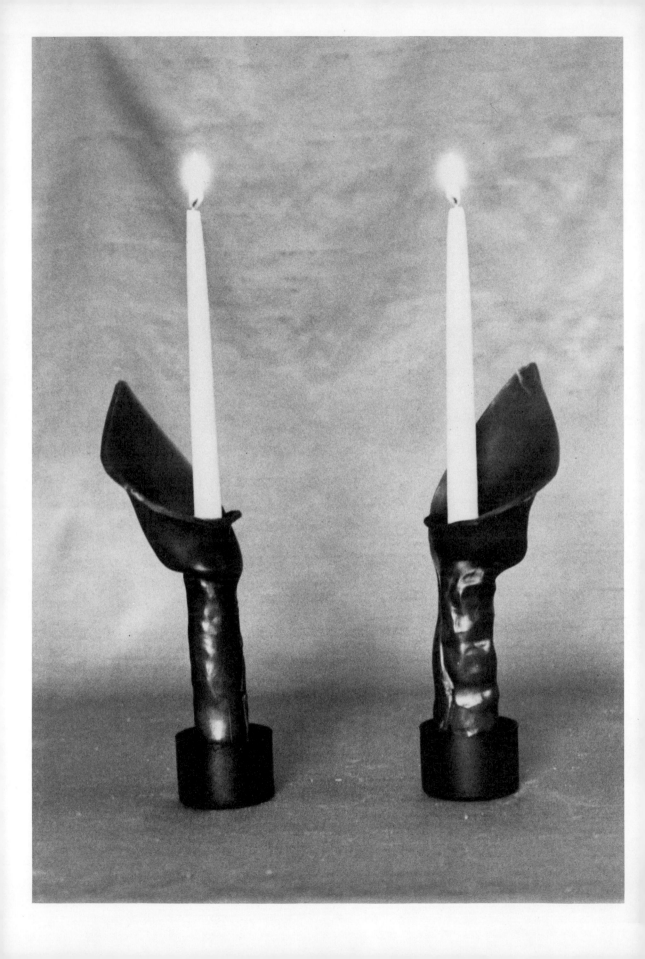

Rolled Candles

Rolled candles can be made of store-bought wax sheets, or you can pour your own. Whatever method you use, rolled candles are simple to make and offer unlimited possibilities for creativity. Detailed instructions for making rolled candles are on page 144.

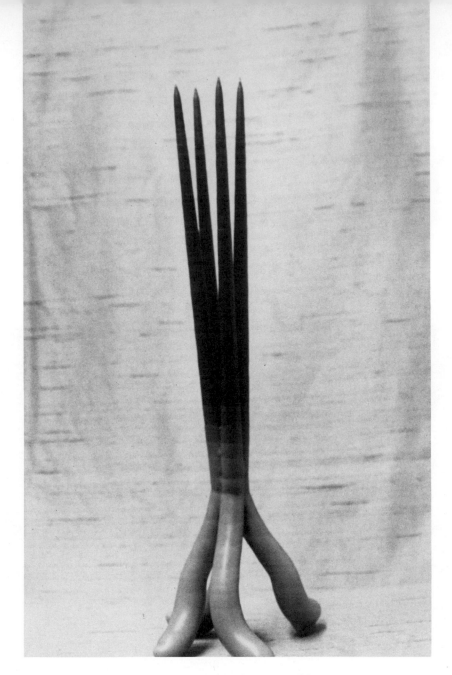

Spear-tipped Candle

Heat and soften the lower portion of long tapers in water at 125–135 degrees. When they are pliable, bend and shape the tapers and stand them up on end. Form a pedestal by placing the bent tapers in a bowl or container filled with hot wax. Remove from the container when cool. If you wish, carve the container-shaped base to resemble an abstract sculpture.

Trees

Cut lengths of poured wax and roll each around a wick. Twist and intertwine a number of these rolls into tree shapes. Secure them on a firm base, preferably one sculptured from the same wax.

Draped Candle

Draped candles are made by draping or molding a sheet of
warmed wax over a taper. See detailed directions on page 140.

Dye Design

Pour hot colorless or pastel-colored wax into a mold. When a film begins to form on top of the wax, sprinkle powdered candle dye on the surface or drop small, solid pieces of colored wax into the mold. The color leaves streaks as it makes its way to the bottom, and when the candle solidifies the colors will show through.

Another way to achieve the same design is to pour the wax, and when a 1/8-inch shell is formed around the inside wall of the mold, pour out the excess wax. Then sprinkle or press powdered dye into the warm shell, let it dry and refill it with cooler wax.

Remember, the basic color should always be clear or a very pale pastel. The design dye must be a darker, more vivid color. Reversing the color scheme will not produce the proper effect.

Chunk Candles

Chunk candles are made by placing colored-wax chunks into a mold and then pouring a low-temperature wax over them to form the shape of the candle itself. Detailed instructions for making chunk candles are on page 135.

Drip Candles

Drip candles are created by taking a blank candle of virtually any shape and slowly dripping an especially-prepared drip wax over it. Prepared drip waxes are available in many colors at craft shops.

Melt the drip wax to 150 degrees in a small container, preferably one with a spout. If you want to use more than one color, melt each color in a separate container. Place the blank candle on a piece of aluminum foil or in a pan and pour the drip wax from the top, letting the colors drip slowly down the side of the candle. Keep rotating the candle as you work.

If you want a thin dribble, use a hotter wax and apply the wax with an aluminum meat baster or a fine-spouted vessel. For large, pebbly drips, use a cooler wax. For an unusual effect, invert the candle and drip the wax toward the wick.

Rainbow Candles

Make blocks or circles of colored wax in any desired thickness. Measure the pouring wax carefully if you wish layers to be the same thickness. Stack one block on top of another with hot wax between each layer. Thread a metal-core wick after the candle is removed from the mold. Dip the candle in a wax/water bath to fuse and blend the colors.

Suggestion: Pour layers of different-colored wax into a mold. Be sure to let each layer harden before pouring the next.

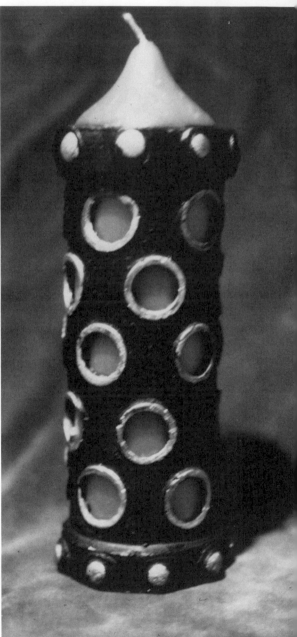

Two-toned Candle

Pour a white or pastel-colored candle. When a thin shell forms around the interior, pour out the excess and let the shell harden. Refill the mold with wax of a darker color at a lower temperature to avoid melting down the first coat. Pour the wax down the center, not against the side as with other candles, to avoid melting the first coat.

Holey Candle

Fill a tall mold with high-temperature melting wax. When a quarter-inch shell forms around the interior, pour out the excess and let cool. Remove the shell from the mold, and with a heated bottle cap or other circular object melt holes in the shell in a predetermined pattern. Then replace the shell in the mold and refill with wax of a contrasting color, at a lower temperature to keep the shell from melting.

Suggestion: Instead of refilling the shell with wax, insert a snug-fitting blank candle of a harmonizing color into the shell. When inserting the candle in the mold, be sure to align the seams.

Marble Candle

This delightful candle is created by using Dip It, a commercial product which can be purchased at craft shops. For detailed instructions for making a marble candle, see page 142.

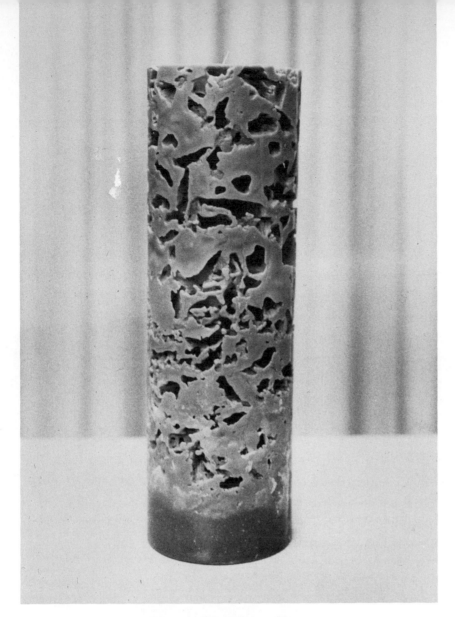

Ice-cube Candle

Invert a large metal mold or milk carton and thread a wick. Fill the mold with ice cubes, using finely crushed ice for small, delicate perforations and larger cubes for more generous holes.

Pour melted wax over the ice at 210–220 degrees. The dissolved ice will leave crevices inside the candle. After removing the candle from the mold allow the excess water to drain off.

Suggestion: Insert a "dripping" candle of a contrasting color as a wick. As the candle burns the drippings will run into the crevices, creating an additional dimension.

Aluminum Foil

Secure a wick in a tall mold, fill it with a deep-colored wax and when a 1/8-inch shell forms around the walls of the mold, pour out the excess wax. Gently pack loosely crumpled puffs of aluminum foil in the center as far away from the wick as possible and refill the mold. Remove the pieces of aluminum foil as the flame reaches the level of the decorations.

Suggestion: Press a votive candle in the center when the wick burns down. This way just the votive will burn, not the entire candle.

Mottled Candle

While mottling is considered a flaw when unintentional, it can be used as a decorative technique. To achieve this effect, a commercial mottling oil is available. Follow manufacturer's instructions, and be sure not to use mottling oil with a low-temperature wax.

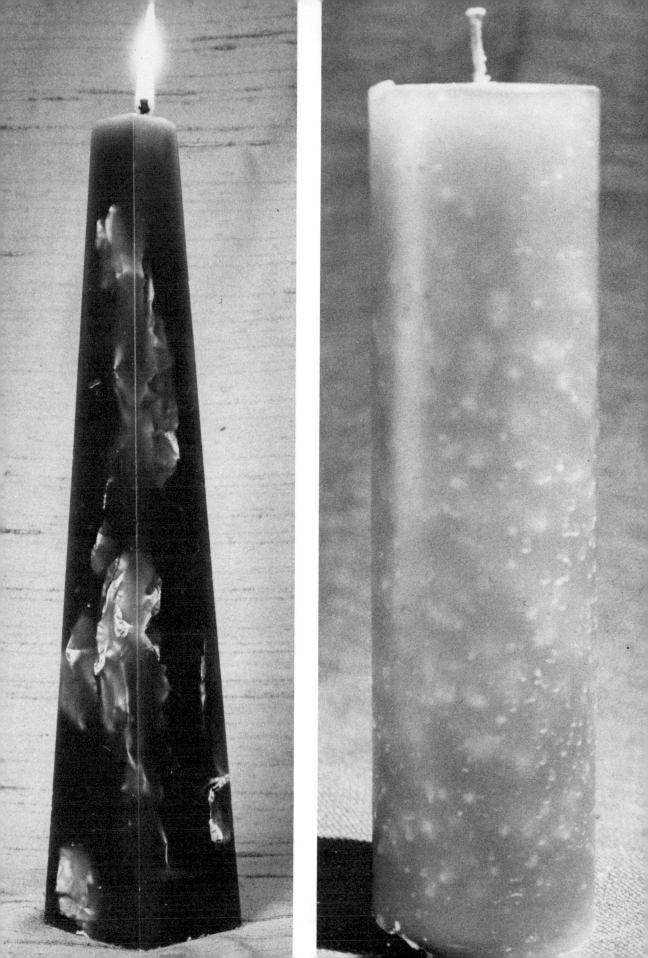

Interior Design

This candle closely resembles the hurricane type, only it is solid instead of hollow.

Pour a large hurricane-type mold, and do not use stearic acid or magic crystals. Pour out the excess when a 1/8-inch shell forms around the interior. Sprinkle bits of color or attach flowers or other decorations to the inside surface and refill the mold. When the wick is partially burned down you may place a votive candle in the center.

PART III
More Candlemaking Techniques

· Chunk Candles ·

Make your own chunks or buy them by the pound or package.

To make chunks: Add stearic acid and color to your melted wax and pour into lubricated ice-cube or serving trays. While the wax is still warm, cut it into small cubes, squares·or triangles, or use fluted bottle caps as designs. Sort the colors into separate plastic bags and store them in a cool place.

To make chunk candles: Stack colored chunks in the mold in a predetermined order, drop them in casually or use a single-colored chunk with a contrasting pouring wax to create a two-toned effect.

Do not add stearic acid to the pouring wax or the candle will be opaque. Pour your wax at a lower temperature than the chunks, otherwise the colors will melt and run together. However, if you wish the colors to blend, then do use a higher-temperature pouring wax.

The heat and pressure of the pouring liquid will push down the chunks, and a number of refillings will be necessary.

Wax chunks.

· Dinner Candles ·

Prepare and wick a multiple mold. Reinforce the bottom against leakage or seepage. Add color and/or scent, if desired, and pour the mold.

Left: Wicking a multiple dinner candle mold.

Right: Pouring a multiple mold.

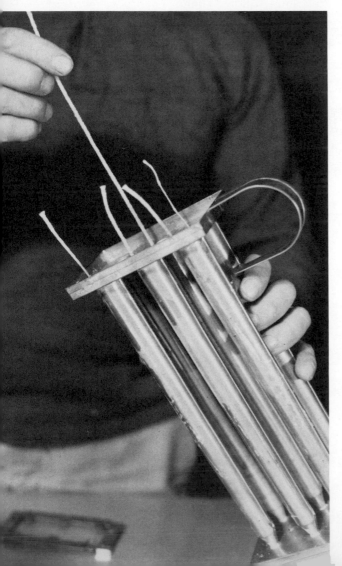 

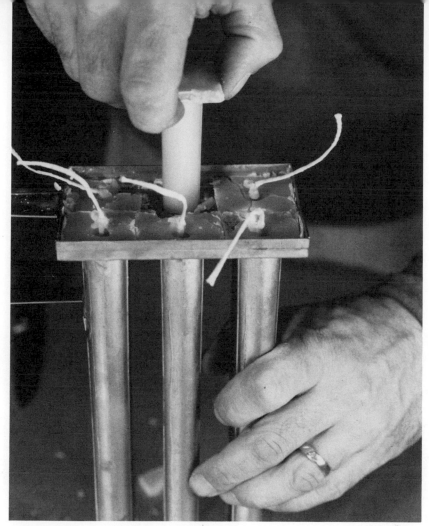

Removing a finished dinner candle.

· Dipped Candles ·

Melt enough wax in a container that is at least two inches taller than the desired candle. Use a medium-melting wax and dip at a temperature of 150 degrees. If too hot the wax will not adhere properly to the wick and will leave bumps on the candle.

Keep a thermometer in your working pot and the temperature of the wax constant; refill the liquid to its original level often for even-sized candles.

Cut wicks to desired lengths, allowing two inches extra for handling and attaching. Space and hang wicks on a rod and tie small dress-maker's weights or washers to the lower ends to keep them straight.

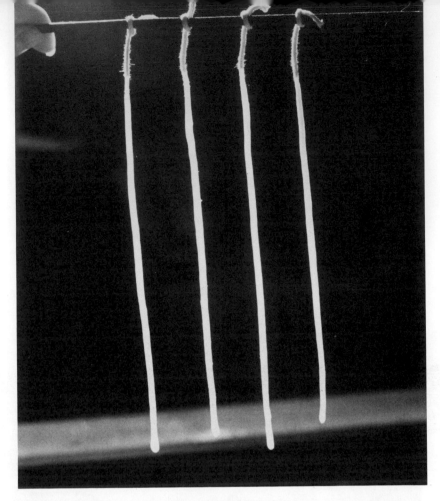

Dipped candles after the first immersion.

Submerge wicks in the heated wax and remove slowly, letting them solidify thoroughly before the next dipping, or it won't adhere properly. Repeat the dipping until the candles are thickened to the desired size.

To attain a uniform candle, keep straightening the wick, watching the temperature and replenishing the absorbed wax often. Do your dipping in a draft-free room.

I prefer hanging my wicks across a rod and placing the rod between two chairs. I bring the wax vessel to each wick, rather than submerging many wicks at once into the vessel. This method takes longer but it eliminates excessive wick motion and produces a smoother taper.

Whichever method you use, your finished candles will still look bowed. Straighten them out when they are cool by placing them on a flat surface. Cover them with wax paper and roll a level board or metal tray over them. Straighten the bottom on a heated skillet or on an inverted cake tin placed in warm water, and cut the wick to a quarter inch.

For added allure, color and scent your dipped candles.

Finished dipped candles.

· Draped Candle ·

Pour a 1/8–1/4-inch layer of wax in a large metal tray. When it is partially set yet "drapable," wrap the wax around a blank candle. Work rapidly, for wax solidifies fast. Let your hands move freely to shape the candle into an unusual form.

Pour wax into a tray. Begin work when the wax is partially set yet "drapable."

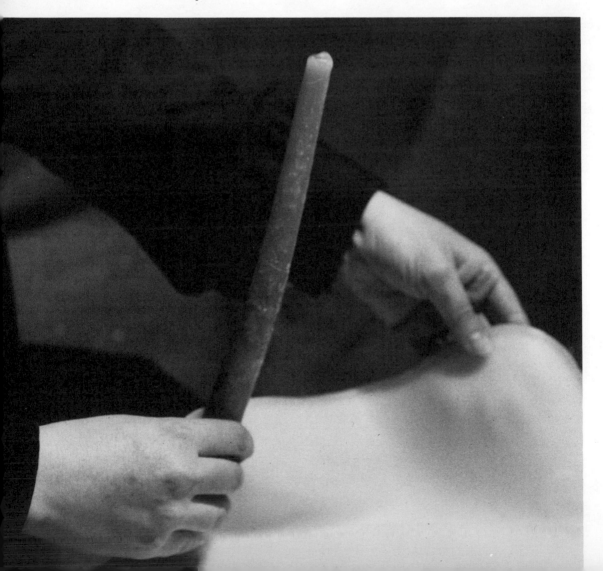

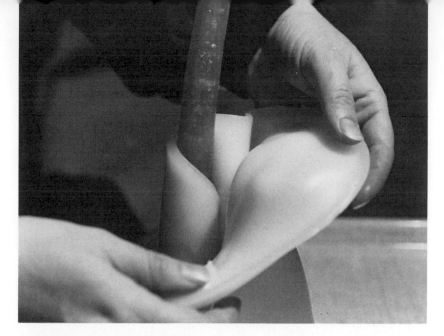

Drape the wax around a taper.

Work with the wax to make a pleasing shape.

· Marble Candle ·

Many unusual effects may be achieved with Dip It, which comes in a variety of colors. Follow the manufacturer's instructions.

1. Fill a pail with water and squeeze a few drops of Dip It on the surface.

2. Stir the water until you create swirls.

3. Immerse the candle by its wick.

4. When the design pleases you, remove the candle and let it dry thoroughly.

To avoid peeling, spray the surface.

Below: Place drops of Dip It in water.

Opposite top: Swirl the dye.

Opposite center: Immerse the candle in the dye.

Opposite bottom: A finished Marble candle.

· Rolled Candles ·

Rolled candles can be made of store-bought wax sheets or you can pour your own. Whatever method you use, rolled candles are simple to make and offer unlimited possibilities for creativity.

WAX SHEETS

Wax sheets come in dimensions of $7\frac{1}{2}$ x 16 inches, in a variety of colors, and are malleable at room temperature. Should the sheets become brittle, soften them on a heating pad, with a hair dryer, or immerse them in hot water. Dry them thoroughly before rolling or water pockets may develop and cause uneven burning.

POURING YOUR OWN SHEETS

Pour sheets of $\frac{1}{8}$-inch-thick melted wax on an oiled cookie sheet or metal tray. To soften wax sheets, use an electric heating pad or place them on a pane of glass over a simmering pot of water.

ROLLING SHEETS AROUND A WICK

1. Lay sheets of wax on a clean, flat surface, using a metal-edged ruler as guide, and cut the wax to desired sizes and shapes.

2. Allowing an extra length for handling, cut a wick and roll the sheet tightly around it to keep out air bubbles and insure longer burning.

3. Press the edges together or flare them.

Variations: Roll one or more sheets around a wick and press designs into the surface with your fingers. Or, cut several different-colored sheets, each $\frac{1}{2}$-inch narrower than the next, stack them on top of each other, the widest on the inside, and roll them around a wick.

Cut wax to the desired size.

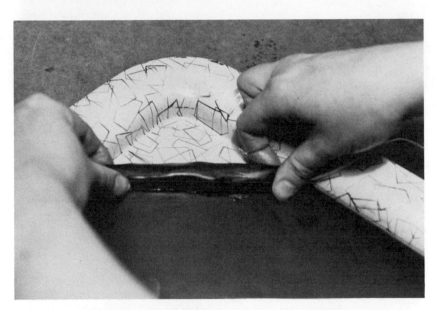

Roll softened wax around a wick.

Press the edges together.

Roll a wax sheet around a taper.

Finish a rolled candle by pressing the edges.

ROLLING SHEETS AROUND A TAPER

Using a taper as wick, wrap a poured sheet around the whole or part of the candle and form it into an interesting design. To create additional unique designs, roll beeswax sheets around the taper.

ROLLED AND CUT CANDLES

Stack several differently colored wax sheets on top of one another and form them into a roll. Cut the roll crosswise into sections and arrange the sections against the interior of a wide mold. Pour clear or harmonizing wax of a lower temperature over them.

Suggestion: Carve into the candle surface with a heated tool to emphasize colors and patterns.

·Wrapped Candle·

You make wrapped candles by pouring wax into a flat decorative rubber mold and, when the wax is set, wrapping the textured decoration around a blank candle.

MAKING YOUR OWN RUBBER MOLD

You can buy rubber molds ready-made in a variety of designs, but if you prefer you can also make your own molds. Find a surface with an interesting texture or design, and make the mold by pouring liquid rubber over the design. Follow the manufacturer's instructions for application of the rubber.

Clean the surface of the mold.

Pour melted wax into the mold.

MAKING THE WAX WRAP

Pour melted wax into the lubricated rubber mold. Remove the wax when it is set and soften it on a heating pad or in warm water when you are ready to use it. Wipe dry, brush craft glue on the back and wrap it tightly around a blank candle.

Trim and fuse the edges with an electric tool. Do not give it a wax/water bath; use a sheen spray or apply Rub'n Buff to bring out the highlights.

Wrap the softened molded wax tightly around a blank candle.

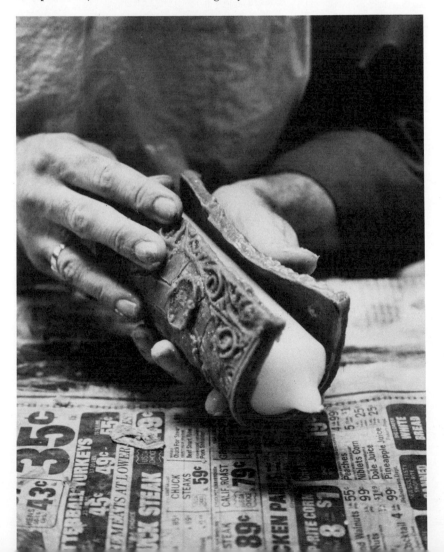

Trim the edges with an electric tool.

Fuse the edges to insure tightness.

PART IV
Appendix

·Where Can I Find It?·

The following is a list of mail-order sources for candlemaking supplies and decorations. Note that you should always write ahead before ordering to inquire about specific merchandise and prices. Many firms also have price lists and/or catalogs.

Artis Incorporated
P.O. Box 68
Temple City, California 91780

Barker Enterprises
15106 10th S.W. Burien
Seattle, Washington 98166

Bersted's Hobby Craft, Inc.
Box 40
Monmouth, Illinois 61462

Cake Decorators & Craft Supplies
Blacklick, Ohio 43004

The Candle Shop
111 Christopher Street
New York, New York 10011

Candlewic Company
2101 Black Horse Drive
Warrington, Pennsylvania 18976

Early American Candle Galleries
Box 100
Trexlertown, Pennsylvania 18087

Florida Supply House
P.O. Box 847
Bradenton, Florida 33507

General Supplies Company, Inc.
P.O. Box 338
Fallbrook, California 92028

General Wax and Candle
Company
Box 9398
North Hollywood, California
91609

The Glow-Candle Company
Box 10102
Kansas City, Missouri 64111

152

Hawthorne House, Inc.
103 North Robinson Street
Bloomington, Illinois 61701

LeeWards
Elgin, Illinois 60120

Lumi-Lite Candle Company
P.O. Box 2, Main Street
Norwich, Ohio 43767

Marjorie's Craft Studio
2620-B West Chester Park
Broomall, Pennsylvania 19009

Natcol Crafts, Inc.
P.O. Box 299
Redlands, California 92373

Novelcrafts Manufacturing
   Company, Inc.
P.O. Box T
Rogue River, Oregon 97537

Hazel Pearson Handicrafts
4128 Temple City Boulevard
Rosemead, California 91770

Peterbrook Incorporated
Candle Mill Village
East Arlington, Vermont 05202

Pourette Manufacturing
   Company
P.O. Box 6818 Roosevelt Way,
   N.E.
Seattle, Washington 98115

Premier Manufacturing
   Company
P.O. Box 26126
Denver, Colorado 80226

A. I. Root Company
1100-06 East Grand Street
Elizabeth, New Jersey 07201

W. Spencer Incorporated
11 Exchange
Portland, Maine 04111

Skil-Craft Corporation
325 West Huron Street
Chicago, Illinois 60610

Wooley & Company
Box 29
Peoria, Illinois 61601

Yaley Enterprises
358-D Shaw Road
South San Francisco, California
   94080

Chemical Supplies: Dyes, Scents, Silicone Rubber, etc.

A-I Plastics of Houston
5822 Southwest Freeway
Houston, Texas 77027

Beacon Chemical Company, Inc.
244 Lafayette Street
New York, New York 10012

Felton International, Inc.
599 Johnson Avenue
Brooklyn, New York 11237

Gardner Associates
1485 Bay Shore Boulevard
San Francisco, California 94124

Great Lakes Solvents Company
1750 North Kingsbury
Chicago, Illinois 60614

Magnolia Plastics, Inc.
5547 Peachtree Industrial
  Boulevard
Chamblee, Georgia 30005

Wax

Industrial Raw Materials
  Corporation
575 Madison Avenue
New York, New York 10022

The Norac Company, Inc.
American Wax Division
405 S. Motor Avenue
Azusa, California 91702

The Norac Company, Inc.
  (Eastern Division)
American Wax Division
169 Kennedy Drive
Lodi, New Jersey 07644

Frank B. Ross Company, Inc.
6-10 Ash Street
Jersey City, New Jersey 07304

Wicking

Atkins and Pearce Company
Pearl & Pike Streets
Cincinnati, Ohio 45202

Decorations

Harrower House
37 Carpenter Street
Milford, New Jersey 08848

· Glossary ·

Aging: the hardening and cooling of a candle before it is removed from the mold.

Beeswax: the wax secreted by bees when they make the honeycomb. It gives off a pleasant aromatic fragrance, is long-burning but expensive. Beeswax was one of the earliest natural waxes used for making candles.

Blank, or core: a blank, or core, is the everyday dinner candle when it is used as a wick.

Color dyes: especially prepared dyes for coloring candle wax. They come in liquid, powder or solid-pellet form.

Flashpoint: the temperature at which an inflammable material catches fire.

Foliation: the formation of heated wax into leaflike or curled designs.

Glitter: shiny, metallic-looking granules that come in a variety of colors, used for decorating candles.

Glitter glue: tubular or spray glue with glitter in it.

Leveling: a technique to make the bottom of a candle even. To level a candle, rotate the base on a heated surface such as an electric hot plate.

Magic crystals: a wax additive, known to the trade as "crystals," which produces a hard, opaque, glasslike finish and improves the burning quality of wax.

Melting point: the temperature at which wax changes from a solid to a liquid state.

Metallic tape: a self-adhering tape that comes in several colors and is used for decorating candles.

Mold: a hollow form in which a candle can be made.

Molded designs: small wax decorations molded in forms that come in a variety of shapes.

Pouring temperature: the temperature at which wax should be poured into a mold. The pouring temperature is determined by the type of wax, the type of candle one is making and the material of the mold being used.

Refilling: the adding of wax to the center cavity around the wick. The cavity is created by the shrinking of the wax during cooling.

Rub'n Buff: a brand name for a metallic paste that comes in a tube. It is used for highlighting designs and decorations on candles.

Sheen spray: a spray (either a commercial candle spray or a clear shoe-polish spray) used to provide a sheen on the surface of a candle. It can be used instead of the wax/water bath.

Sodium silicate: a chemical substance used for fireproofing candle decorations.

Spermaceti: a solid, waxy substance obtained from the sperm whale and used for making candles. It is odorless and does not soften or bend easily.

Splaying: the sloping, slanting or spreading out of the wax around a candle when it is burned.

Stearic acid: a white crystalline substance derived from animal and plant life. It makes paraffin harder, more opaque and longer-burning. It also gives a candle a smoother finish and a more brilliant color.

Stringing: the inserting and securing of the wick in a candle.

Stripping: the removal of a mold in which a candle was poured, especially a milk carton.

Tallow: animal fat extracted by melting, used in making candles, soap, oleomargarine, etc.

Vegetable wax: any waxy product secreted by various plants. The wax from the bayberry shrub or tree, first used by American colonists, is one of the most widely used vegetable waxes.

Votive: a small, stubby candle that usually burns in a container. Originally used for religious purposes, it is now popular in candle-making both as a source of light and as a decoration.

Water bath: a technique for insuring easier removal of a candle from a mold and a smoother, more professional finish on the surface of the candle. The water bath consists of a large container such as a pail or wastebasket filled with lukewarm water. A poured candle mold is immersed into the bath and remains there until the candle is thoroughly set.

Wax: any of various substances of plant or animal origin containing esters and free fatty acids, free alcohols and higher hydrocarbons including beeswax, spermaceti and vegetable wax. Waxes are harder and less greasy than fats.

Wax myrtle: a shrub or tree, also known as bayberry or candleberry, which has aromatic foliage and small, hard berries covered with a coating of wax used in candlemaking.

Wax sheets: sheets of wax about ⅛ inch thick, made by pouring wax onto a cookie sheet or metal tray. Wax sheets are used for making rolled candles or for making cut designs.

Wax/water bath: a technique in candlemaking to give a smooth, professional finish to a candle. The candle is immersed in hot wax for five seconds and then plunged into ice water. The bath can also be used to touch up old candles or to recolor faded ones.

Wick: a bundle of fibers, loosely twisted cord or cotton threads which draw a supply of oil in lamps or melted wax in candles to be burned. Wicks come in a variety of shapes and sizes and are generally of three types: square-braided, flat-braided and metal-core.

Wick cavity: the hole that forms around the wick as the candle solidifies. It must be refilled slowly with hot wax.

Wick tab: a metal fastener used to hold a wick in place.

Wicking the mold: inserting the wick in the correct position inside the mold.

· Index ·